Dundas, Ontario in Photos, Saving Our History One Photo at a Time

Photography
by Barbara Raué
2012

Series Name:
Cruising Ontario

Book 2: Dundas

Cover photo: 104 King Street West, old Post Office

Dundas, Ontario

Dundas was originally known as Cootes Paradise, named after Captain Cootes of the Kings Royal 8th Regiment and was incorporated as a town in 1847. Its tree lined streets, heritage homes and picturesque downtown reflect the nostalgic quality of the past. Businesses, found in renovated Victorian buildings, were mostly built of limestone or brick after a fire in 1881 destroyed original wooden buildings. Downtown consists of two blocks along King Street West with specialty stores. Fran White, the owner of Heirlooms Bridal Saloon, says the building used to be Hugh Walker's Hardware Store built in 1883. They renovated the building in 1987 but kept the original 14-foot ceilings, wooden floors, long counter and sliding rail ladder. Terraware is a hemp shop where all products are environmentally friendly. Mickey McGuire's Cheese Shop offers a wide selection of cheeses from around the world. Inside the Ukrainian Store there are pirogues, traditional meats and delicious biscuits. The arts helped shape the destiny of Dundas which is home to many artists who have achieved international fame. Off the main street is the Dundas Valley School of Art set in an 1830's one time munitions factory on Ogilvie Street. Learn more Dundas history at the Dundas Museum and Archives on Park Street West. Drive slowly down Victoria Avenue to admire gorgeous stately historical homes. Taylor's Tearoom is a great place to have lunch or afternoon tea. The Keeping Room is a fabulous kitchen shop.

King Street

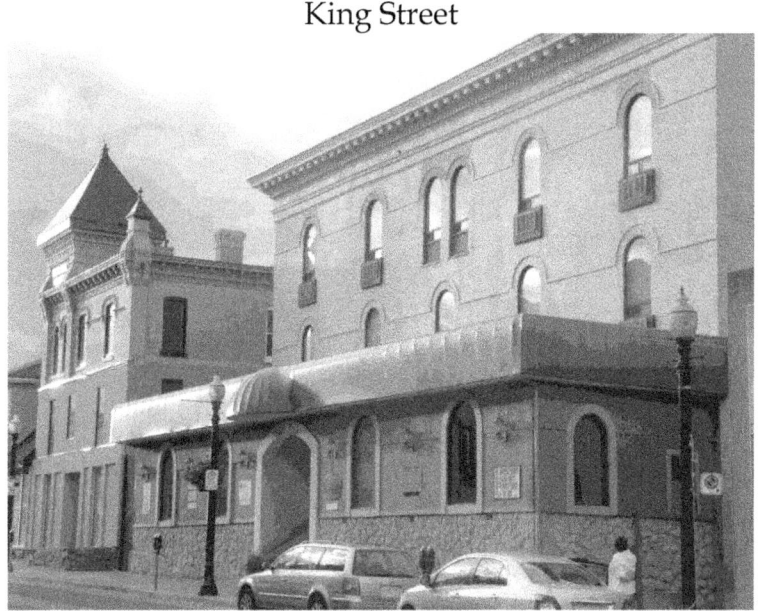

Former Central Hotel

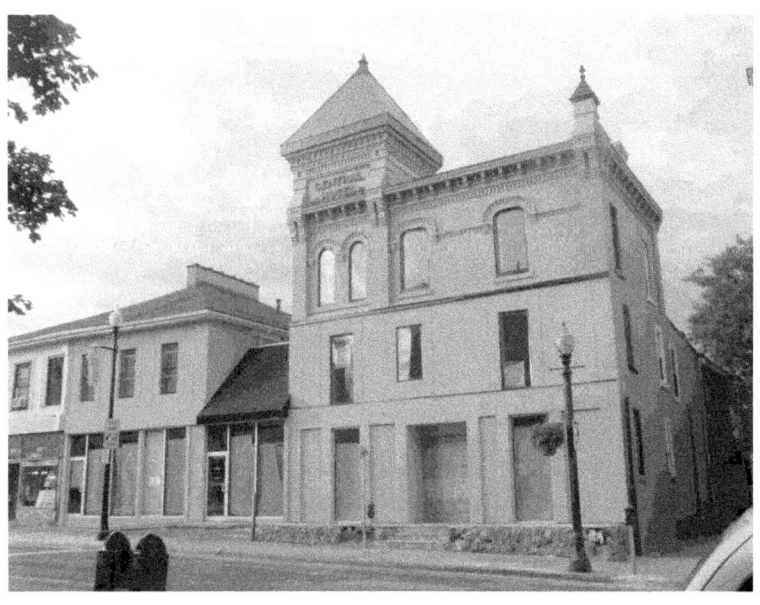

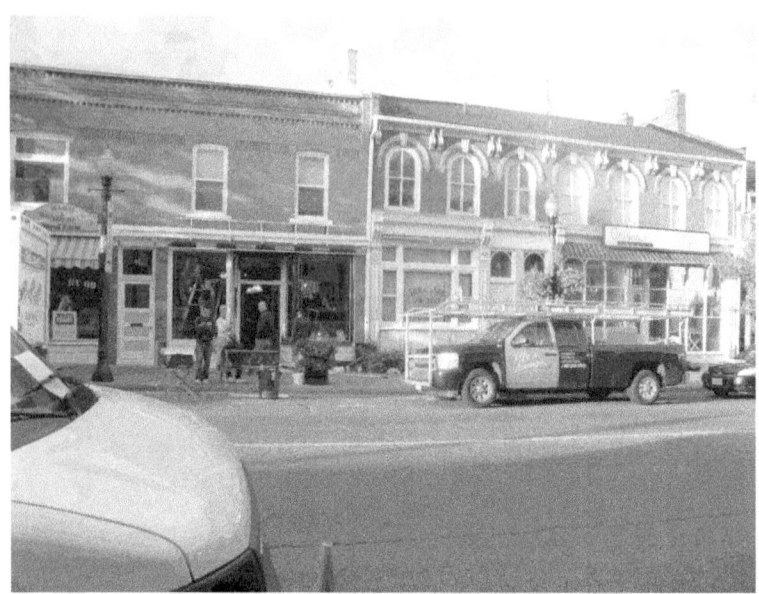

Italianate architecture

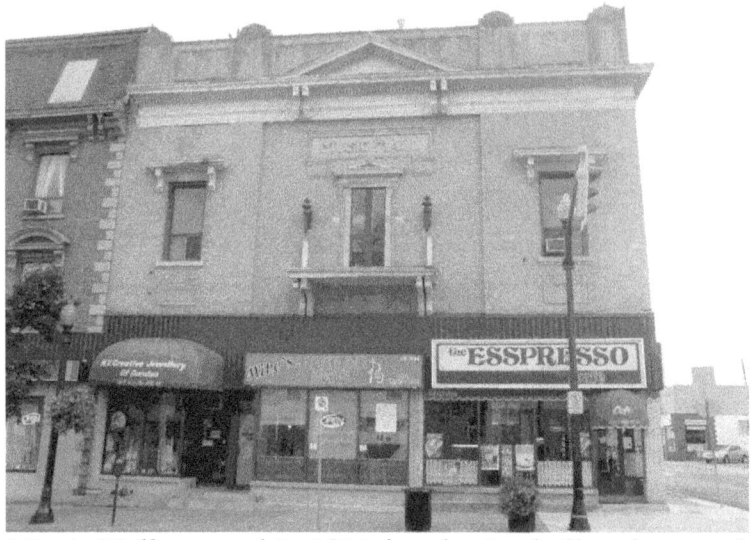

The Music Hall opened in 1911 for charity balls, plays and movies with a seating capacity for 700. Used as classroom space from 1915-1918, it remained vacant from 1966-1977, when it was renovated for mixed commercial/residential use.

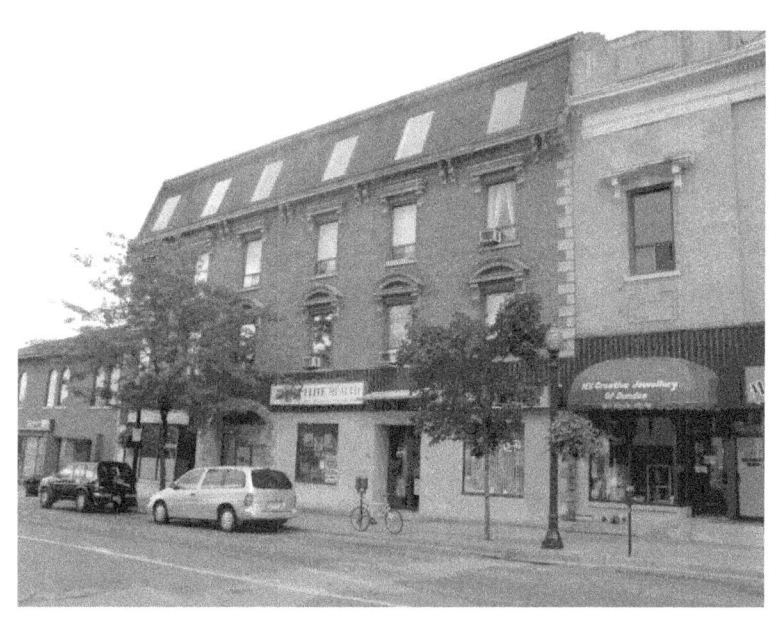

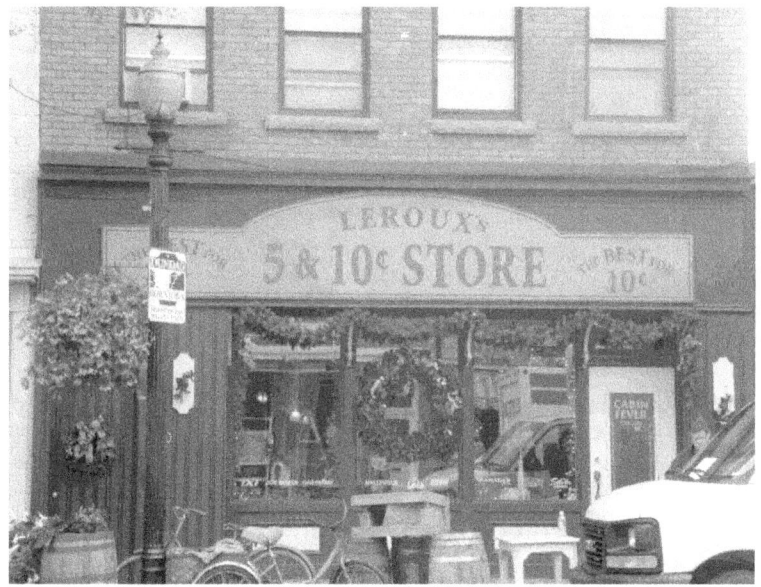

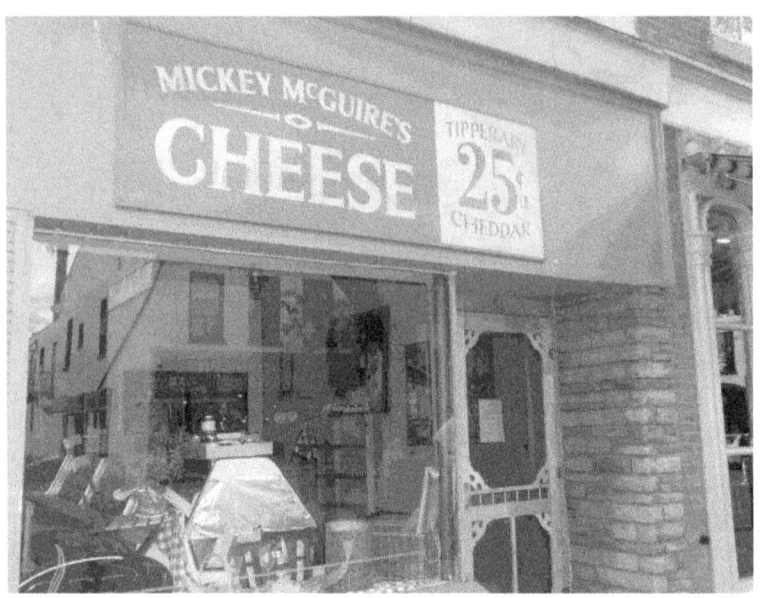

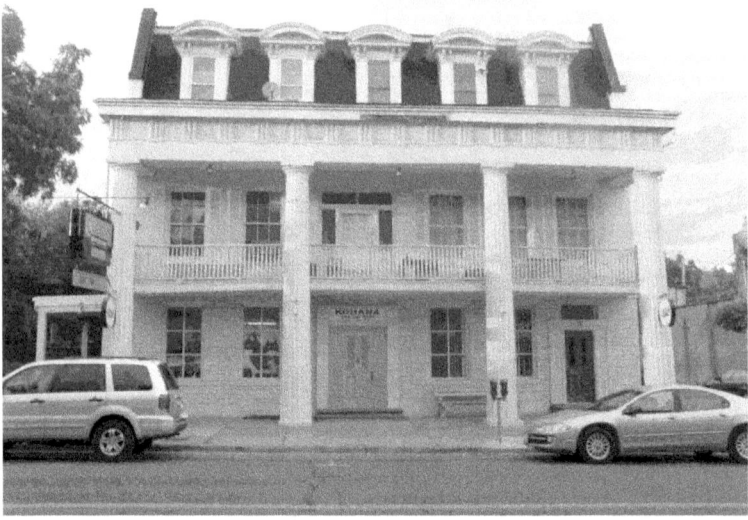

The Collins Hotel, in the Classical Revival style, has a front portico with four fluted Doric columns; the roof has a series of dormers with Florentine pediments. There are two floors to the hotel with a balcony running the full length of the building on the second floor. On the street level there are shops and a restaurant in the back.

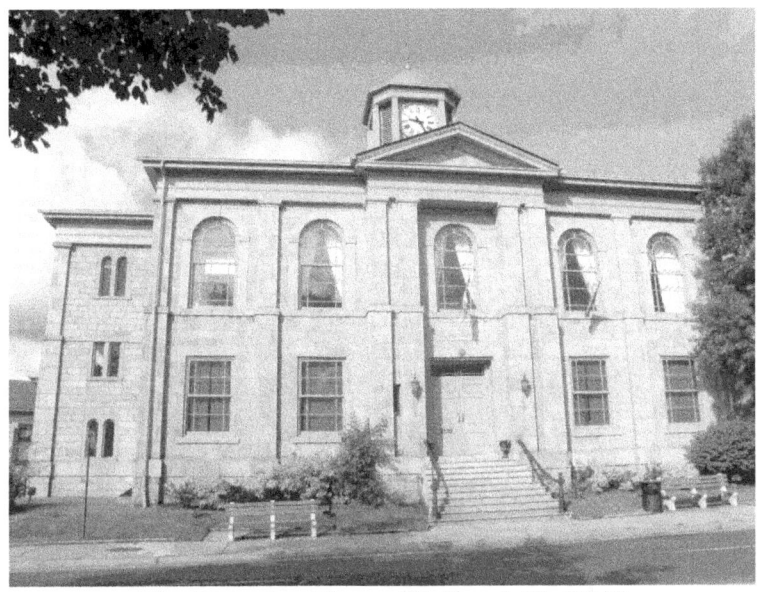

The Dundas Town Hall – A.D. 1848

Dundas was incorporated as a town in 1847 by a special act of the legislature Province of Canada. In 1848, local builder James Scott erected a stone town hall in the Renaissance Revival style. Except for a small Italianate wing added later, the exterior has been little altered, although renovations were carried out in 1946 and 1972. It is made from local limestone with an ashlar finish.

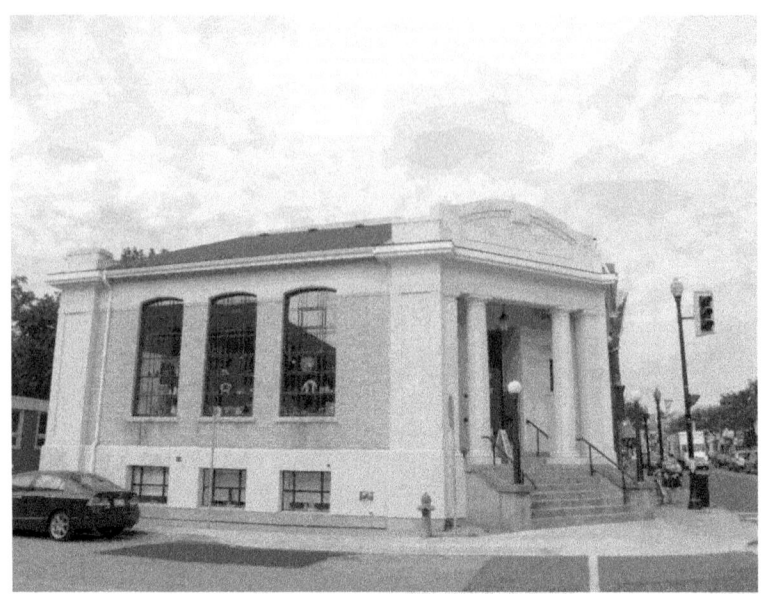

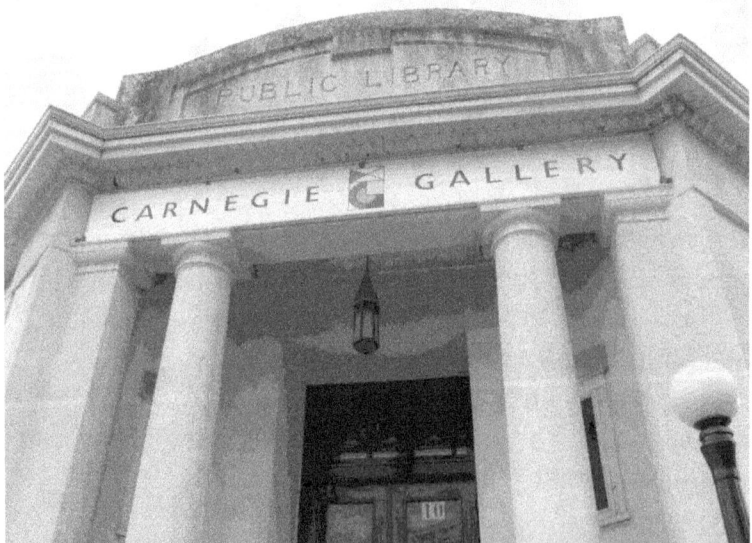

The Carnegie Gallery, once the town library, is an impressive building in the Beaux Arts style with its giant Corinthian pillars, thick fluting, cornice with huge dentils, and nicely carved spandrels. It houses a collection of hand-crafted art objects.

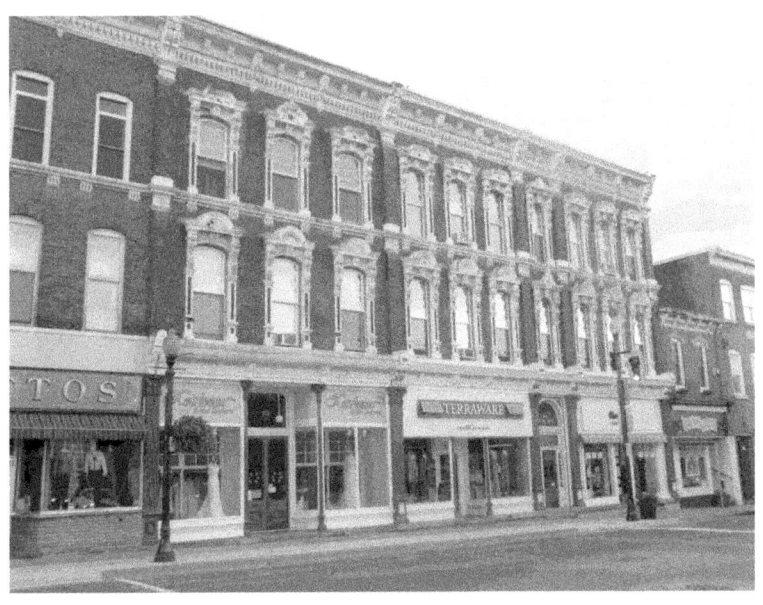

Italianate architecture

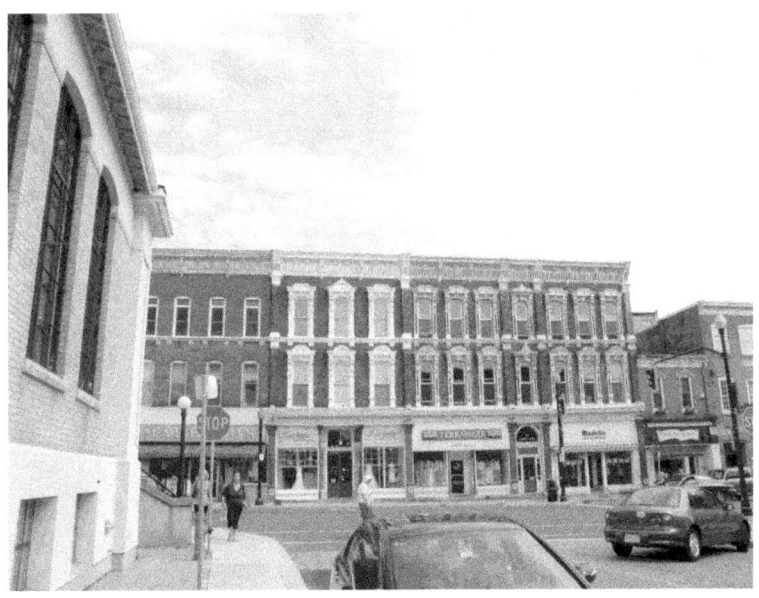

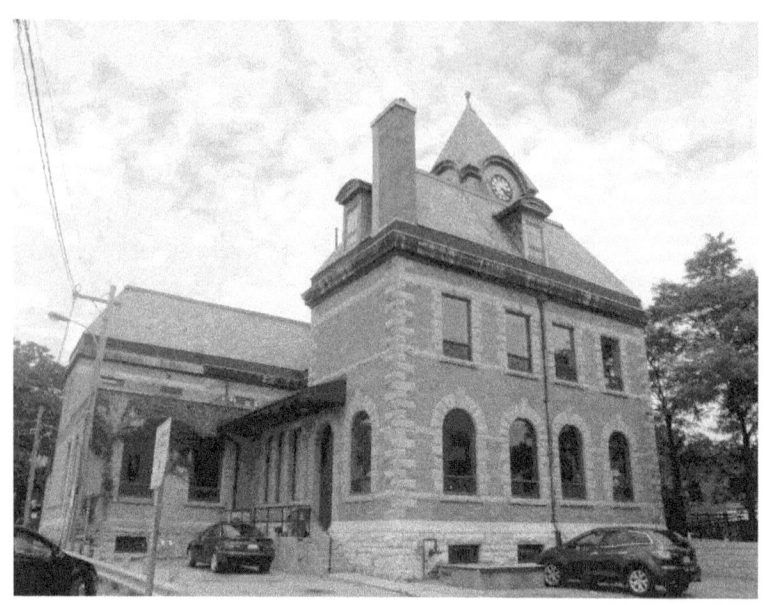

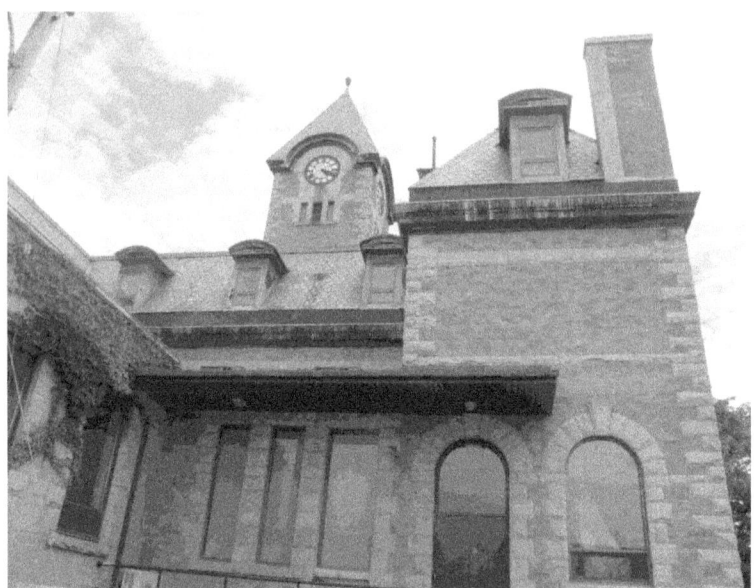

104 King Street West - old Post Office
Built in 1913, the building has a Romanesque façade
dominated by the 100-foot Venetian clock tower, with each
clock face six feet in diameter. The clock was manufactured
and shipped over from England.

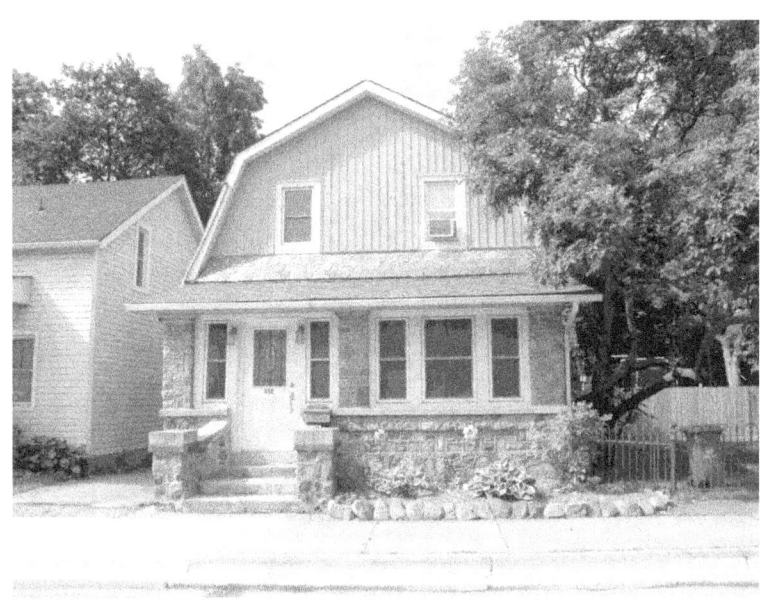

348 King Street West

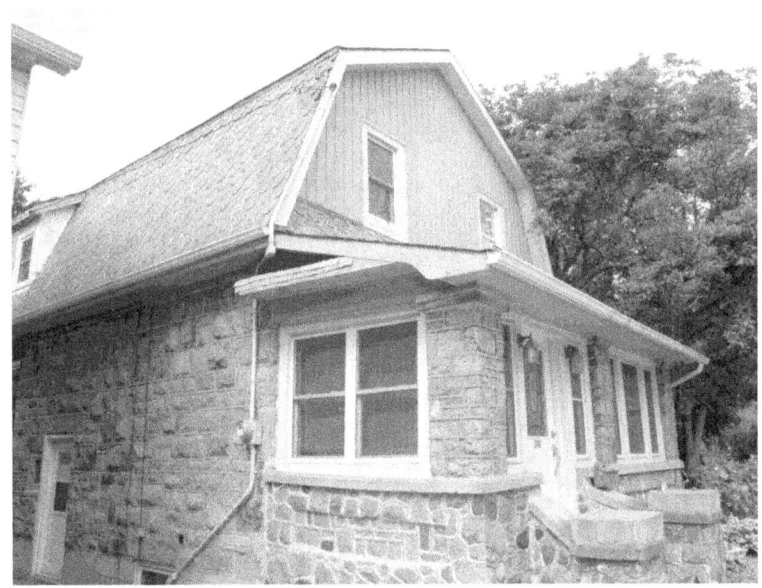

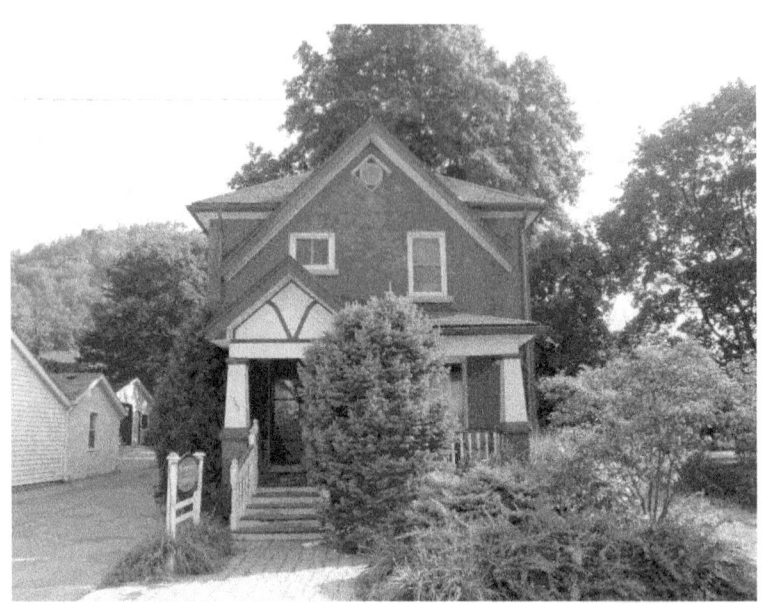

343 King Street West – 1930s construction

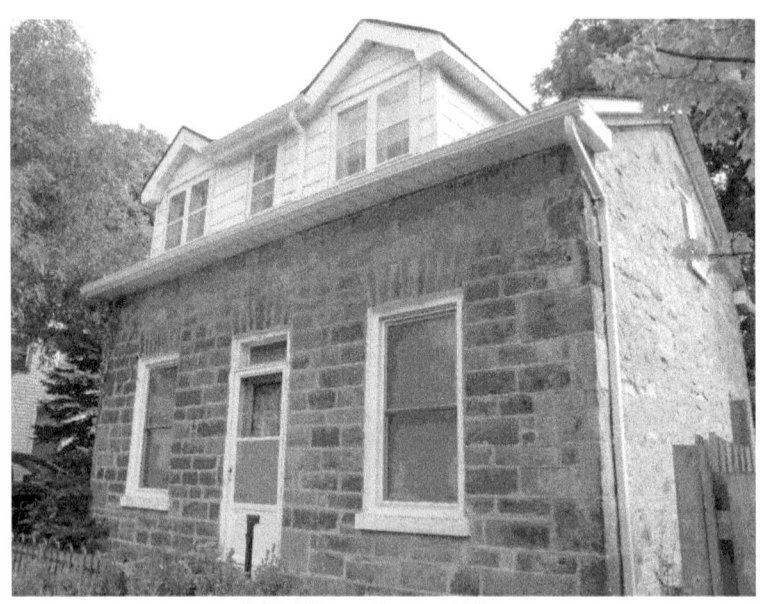

291 King Street West

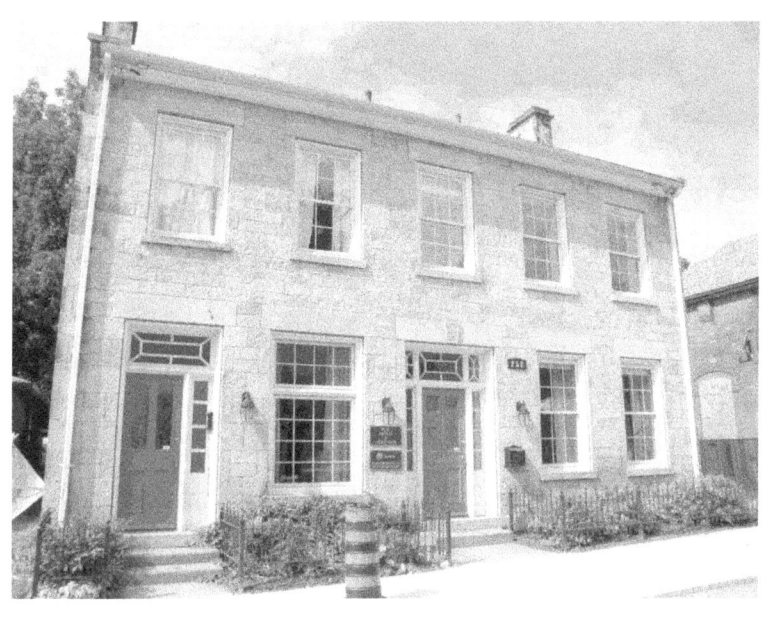

250 King Street West – built in the 1800s

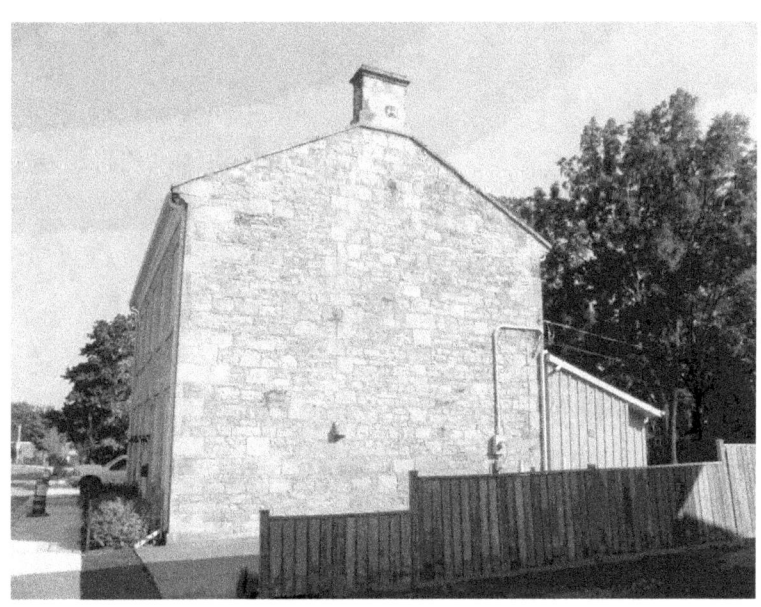

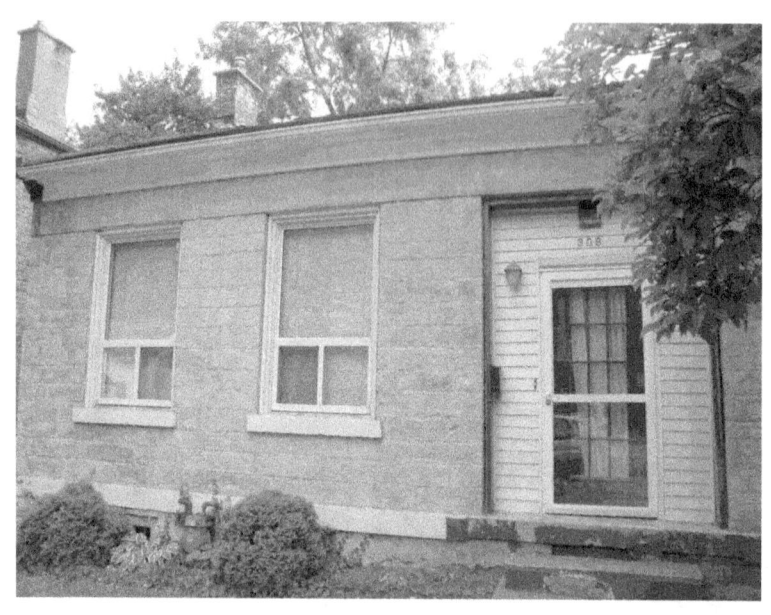

308 King Street West
- old stone house built about 1859

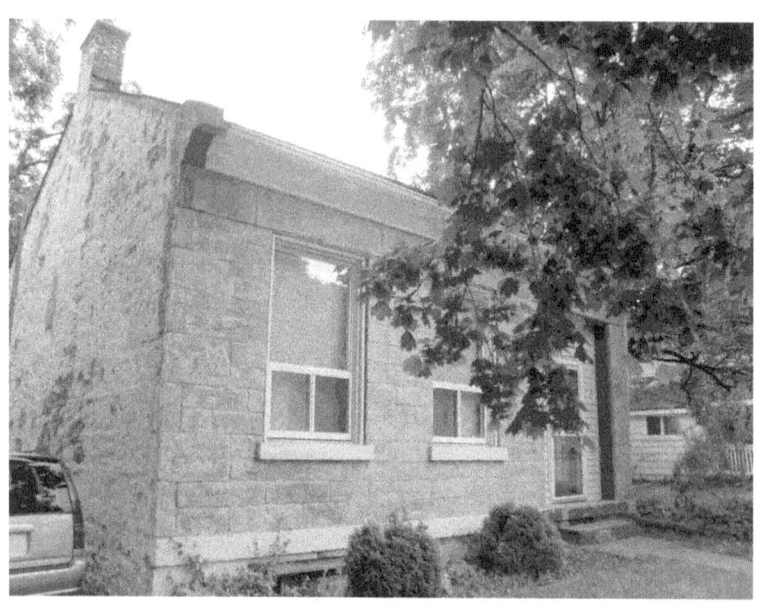

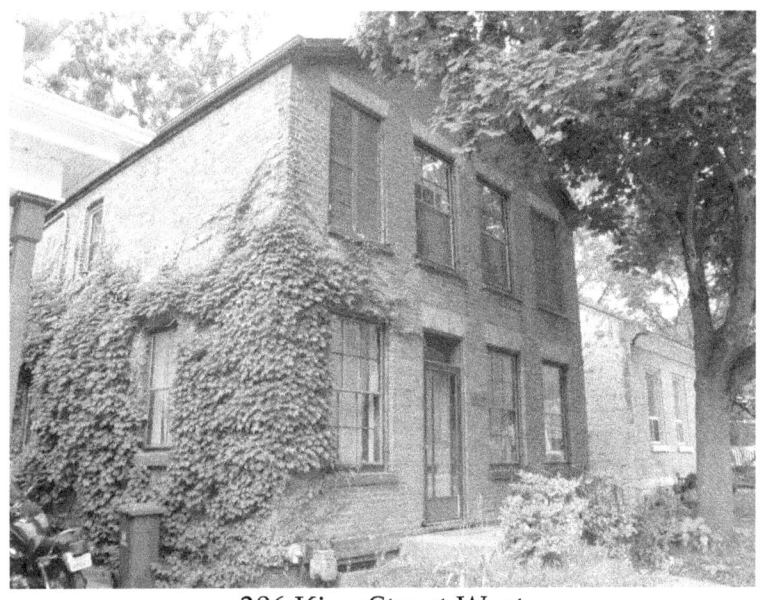

306 King Street West
Note the brick basement – made from bricks from the
local brickworks in operation in Dundas in the 1830s

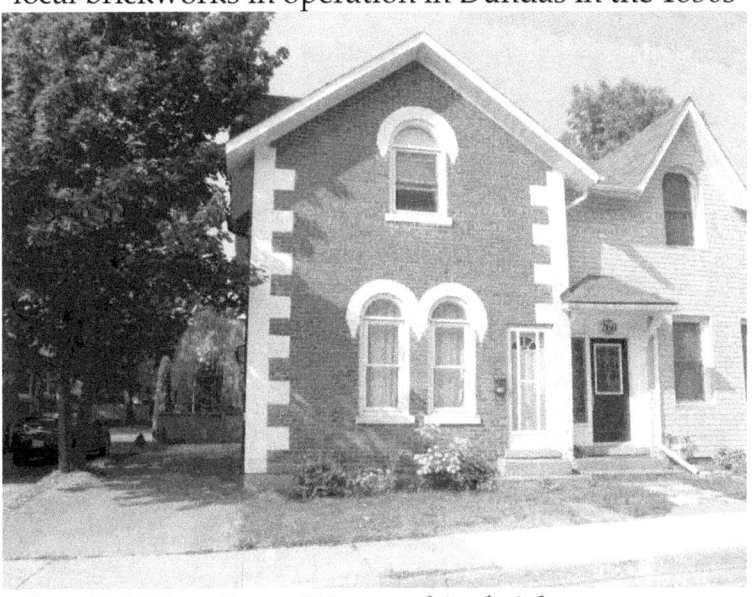

258 King Street West - white brick accents

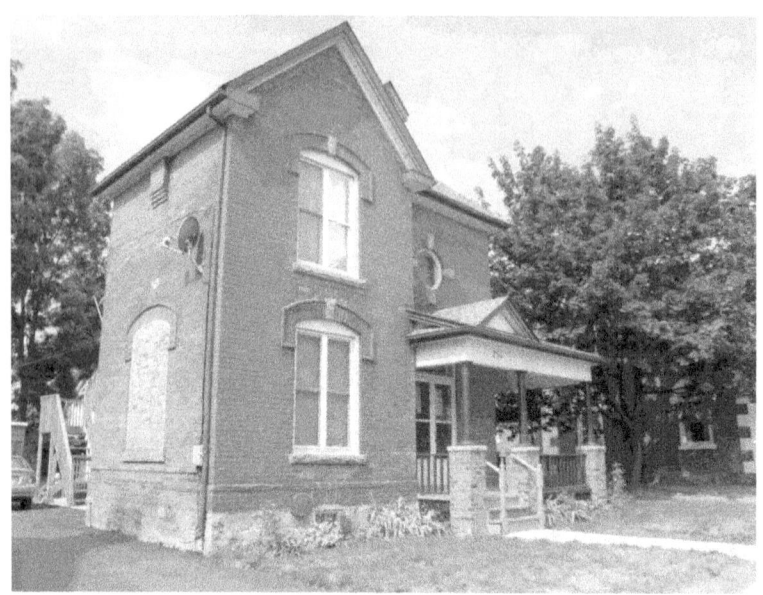

256 King Street West

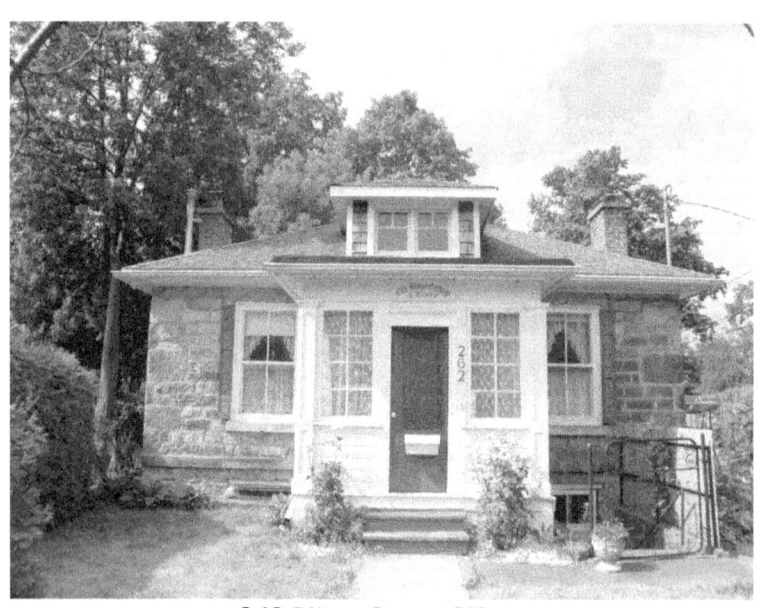

262 King Street West
Old stone cottage 1830

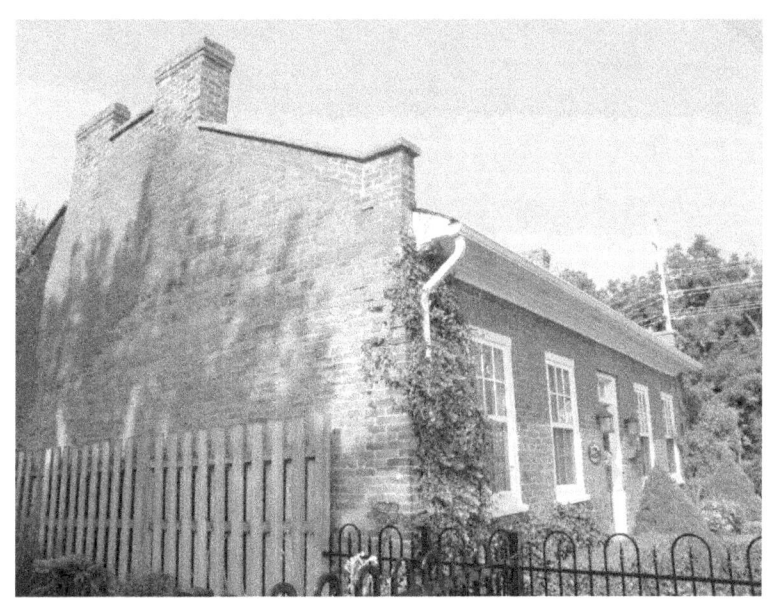

140 Hatt Street – circa 1848
Owned by Gartshore Factory
Pattern-maker, William Kyle
1½ storey vernacular Georgian brick home

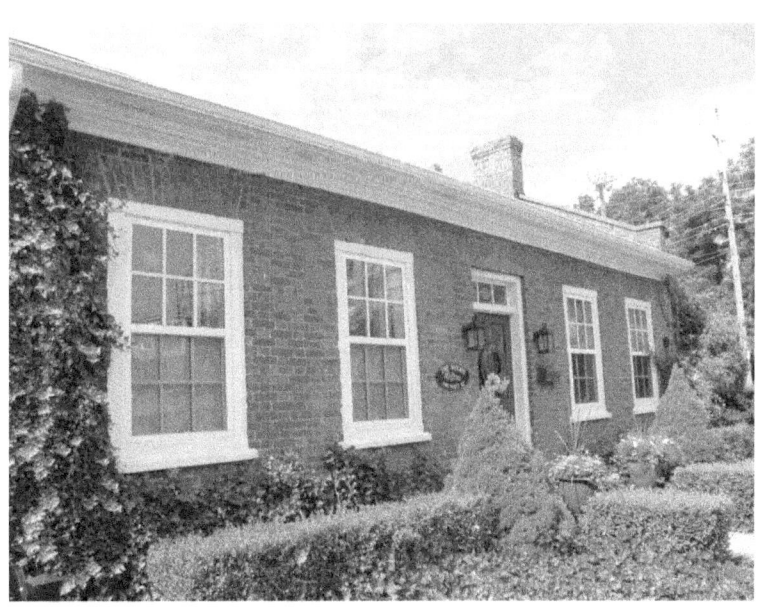

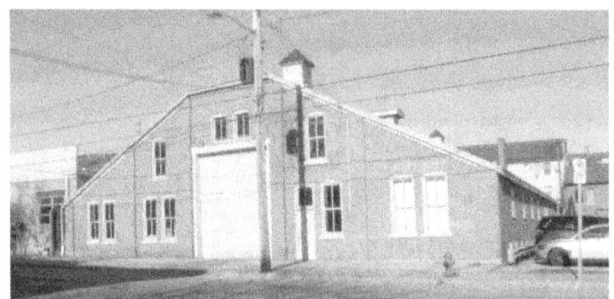

Former bus station

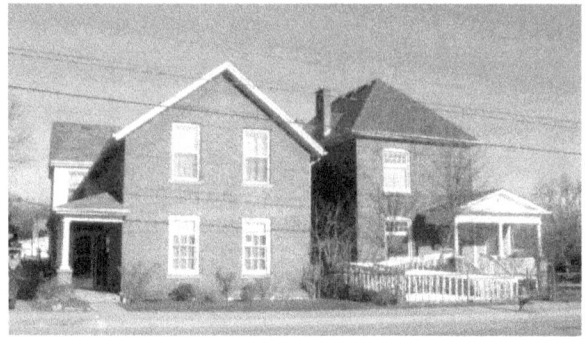

Hatt Street Homes

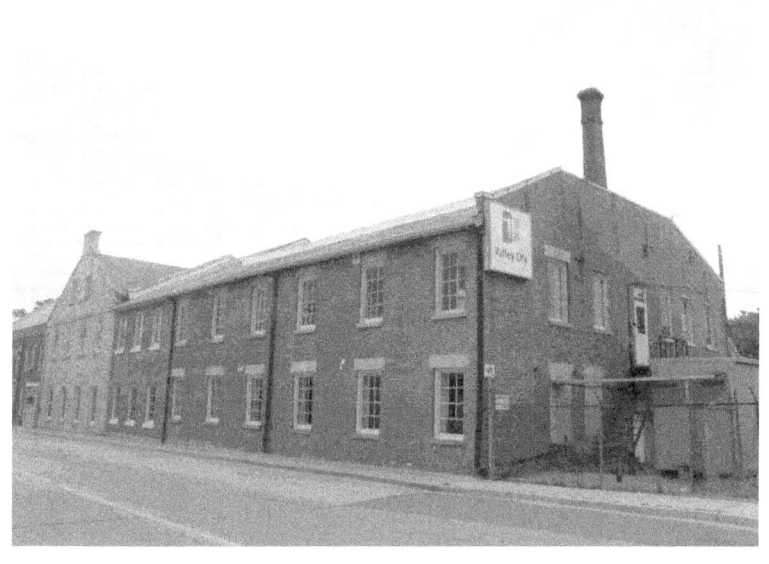

Valley City Architectural Furniture – 1840s – Hatt Street

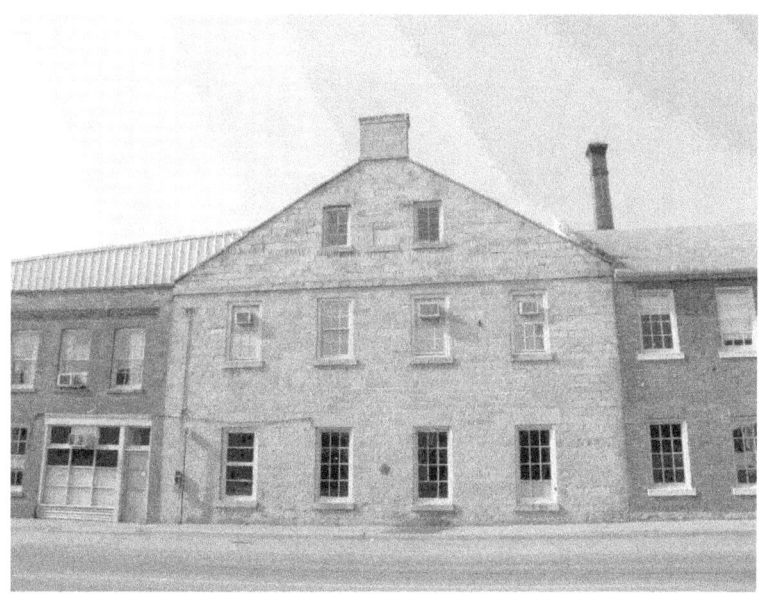

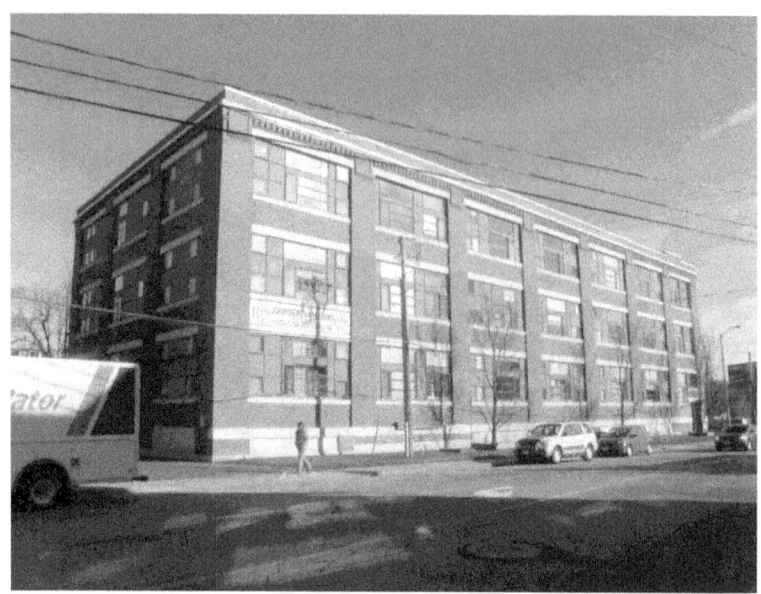

The John Bertram & Sons Company Limited
Tool and Gauge Division – Hatt Street

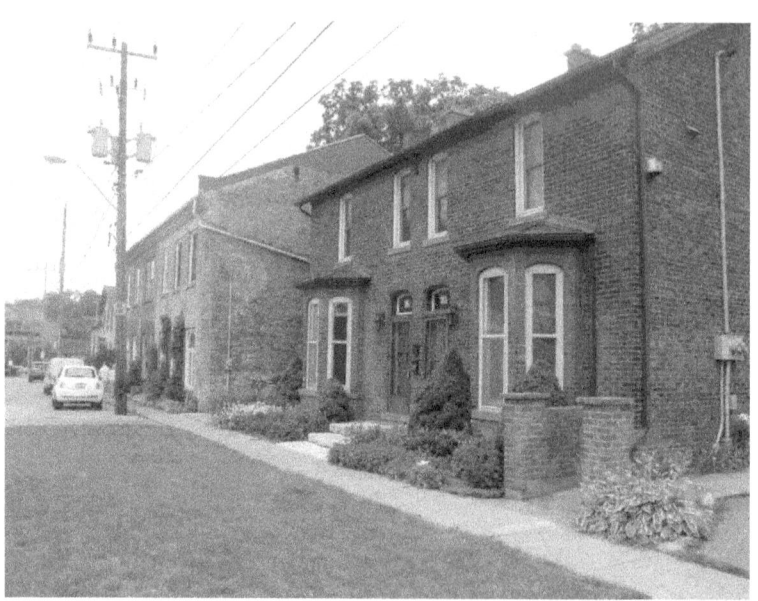

Hatt Street

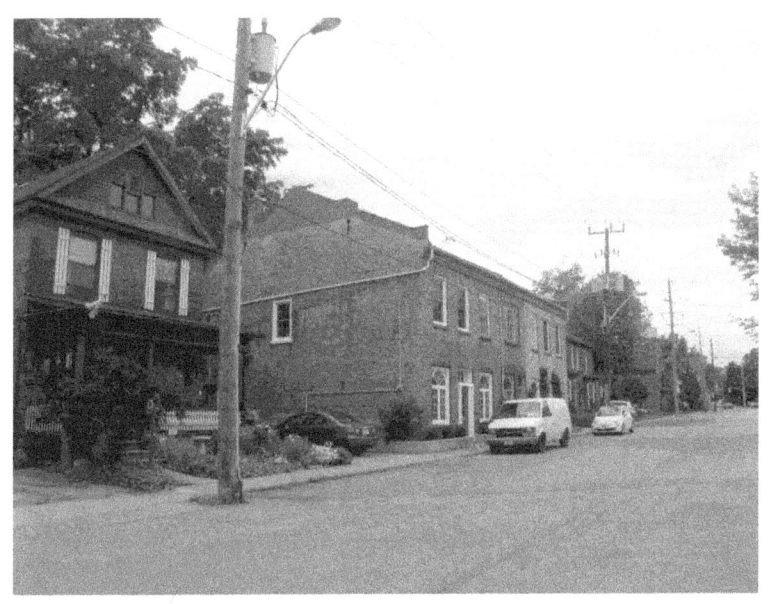

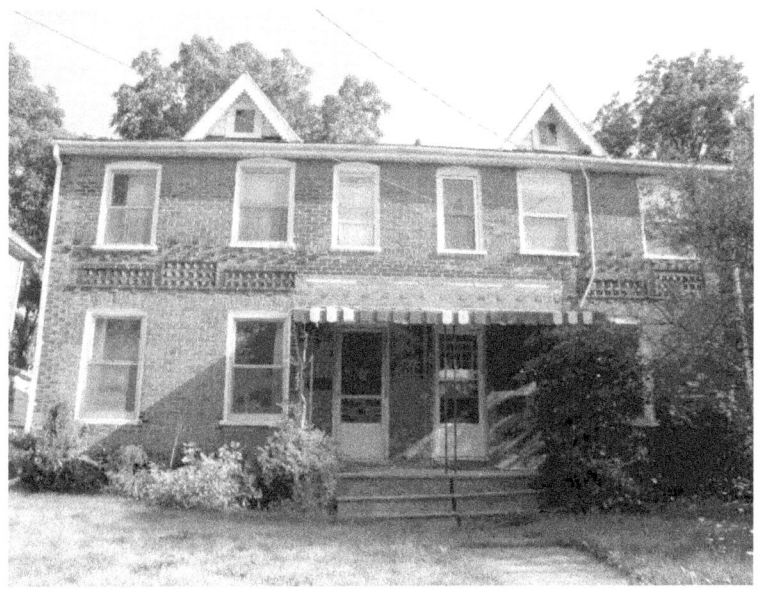

12 and 14 Baldwin Street

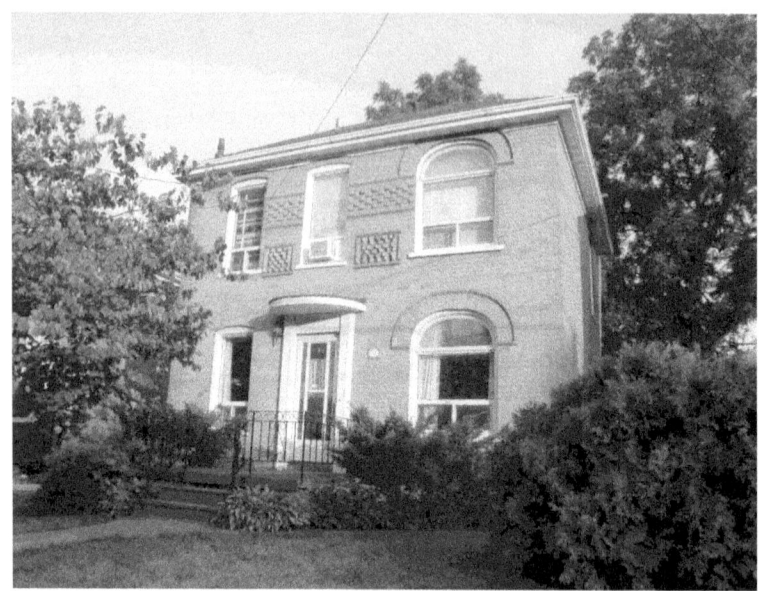

16 Baldwin Street

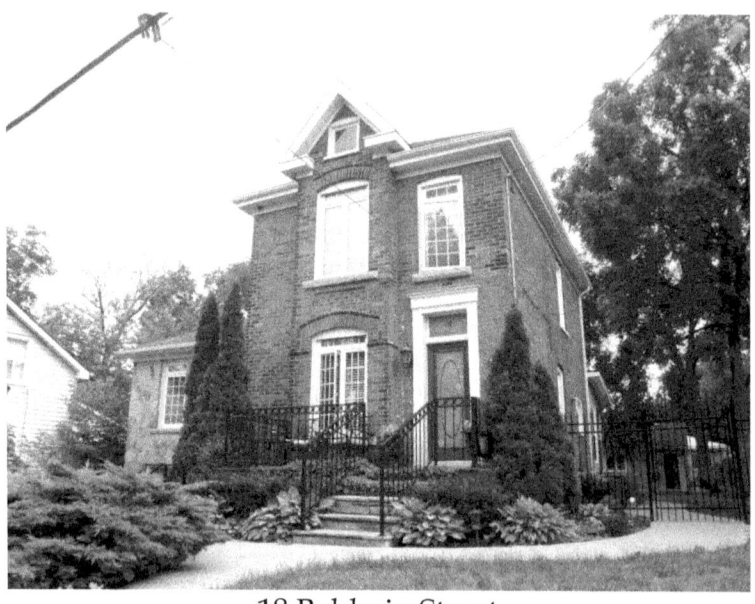

18 Baldwin Street

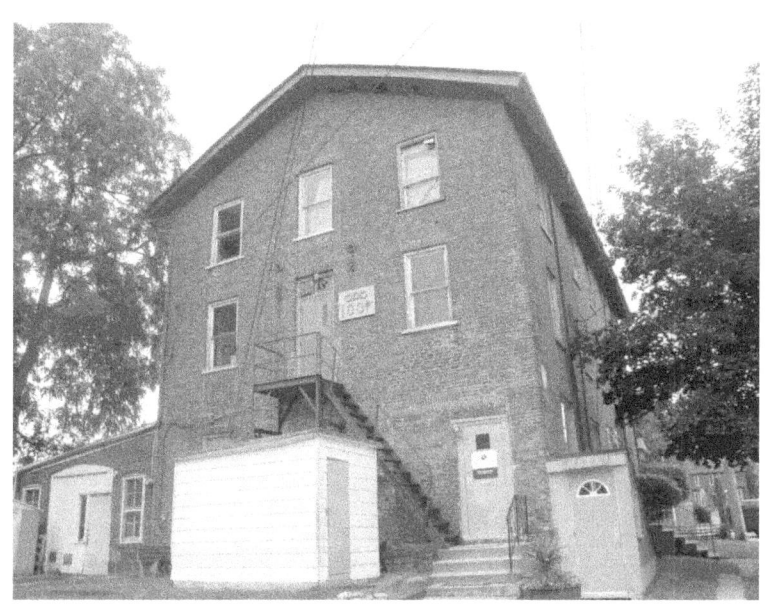

Corner of Baldwin and Main Streets
IOOF – Odd Fellows

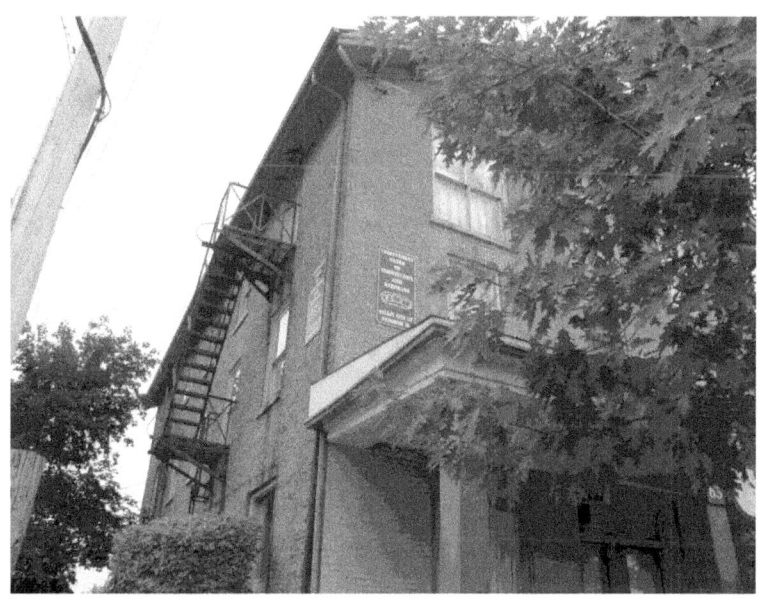

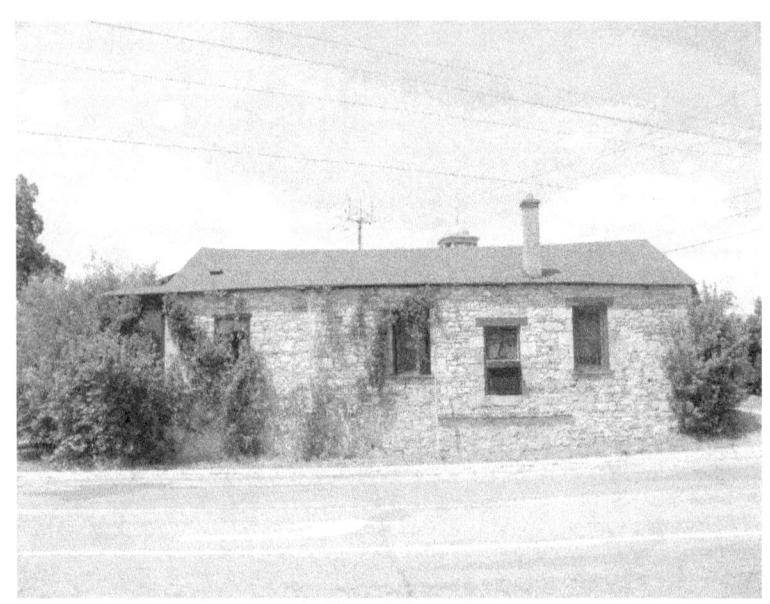

Folkes Electric
on Governor's Road

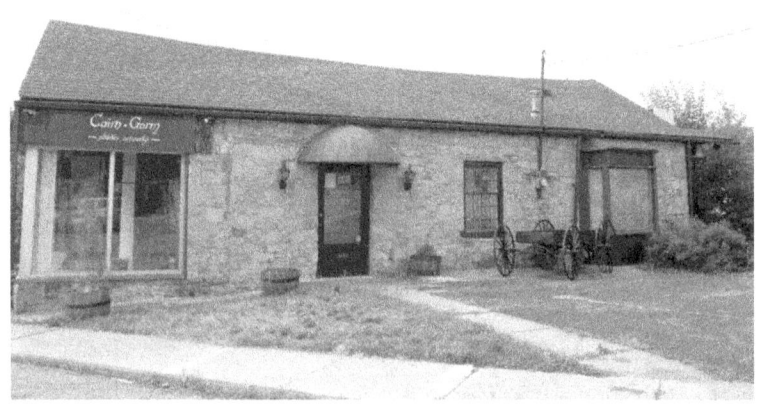

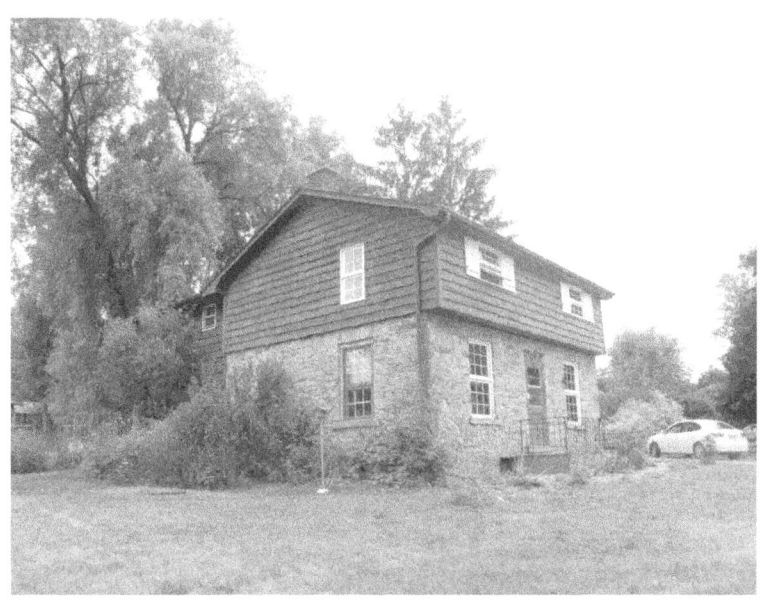

Old limestone house beside entrance to
Dundas Conservation on Governor's Road

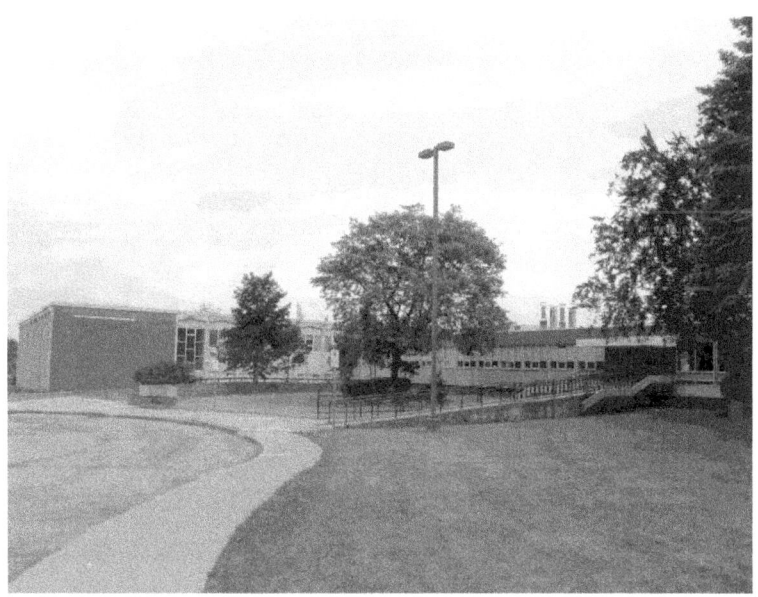

Highland Secondary School, Governor's Road

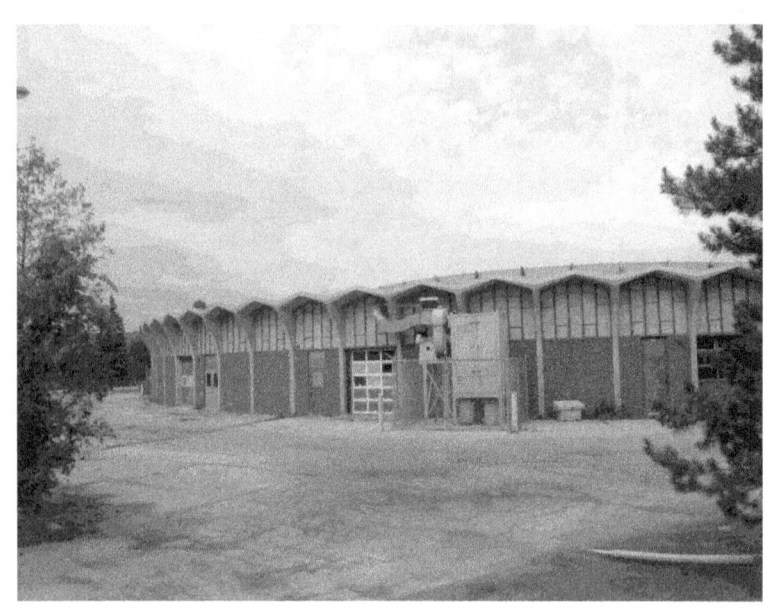

Highland Secondary School

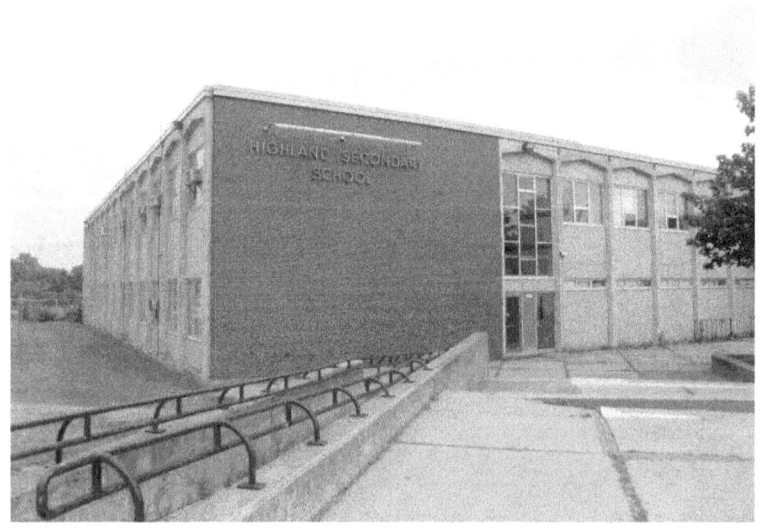

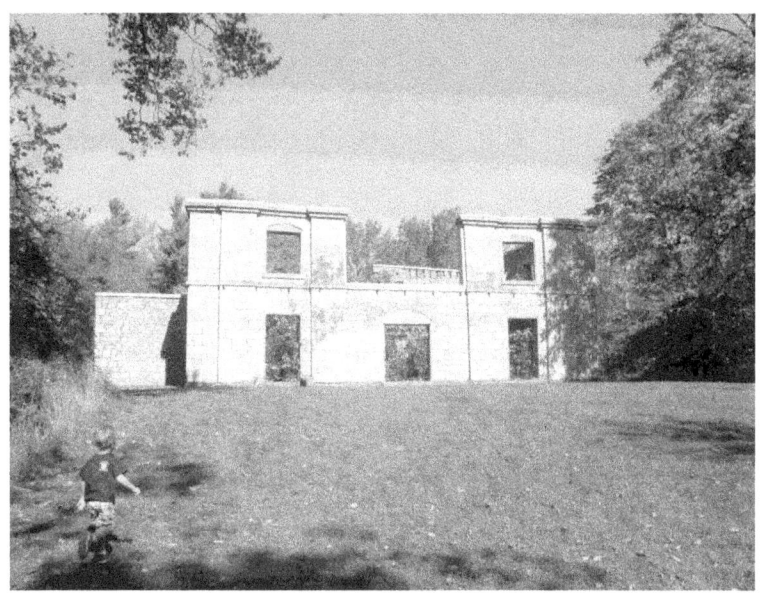

In 1855 George Gordon Browne Leith built the large stone house with limestone quarried on the property. The Leiths used The Hermitage as a summer residence and spent the winters in either Hamilton or Scotland.

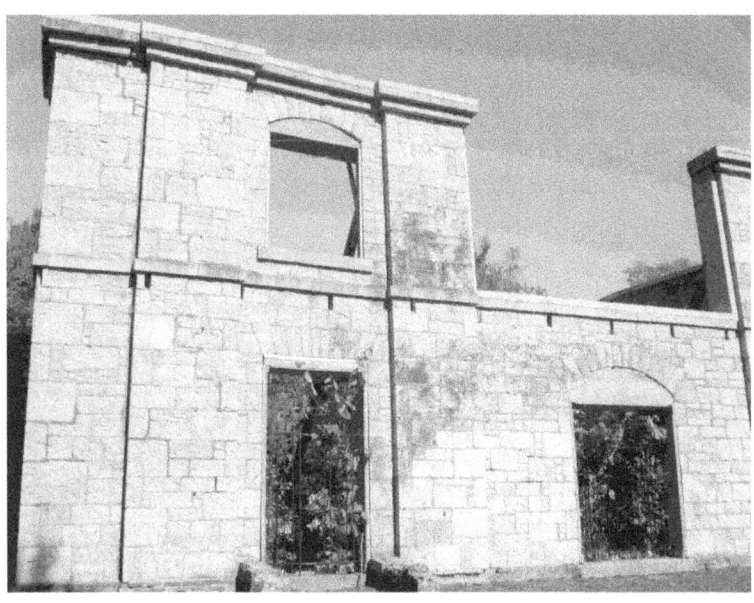

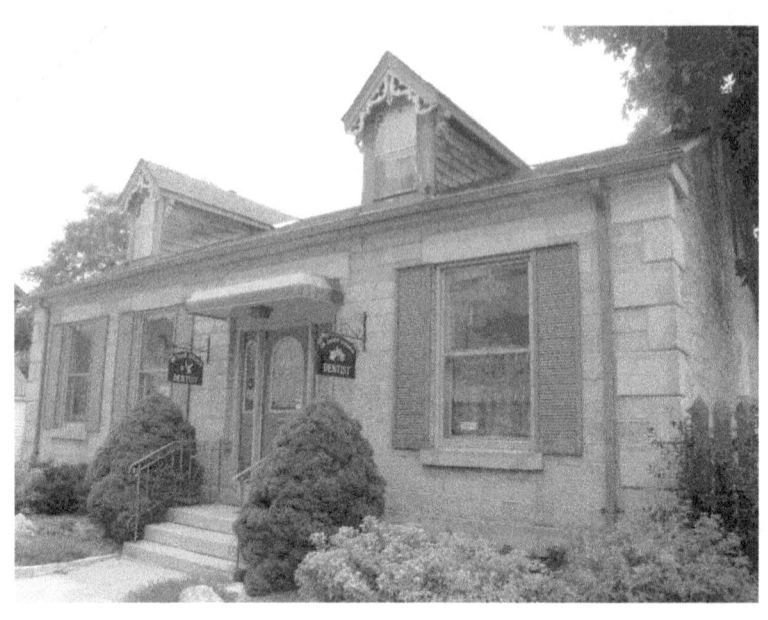

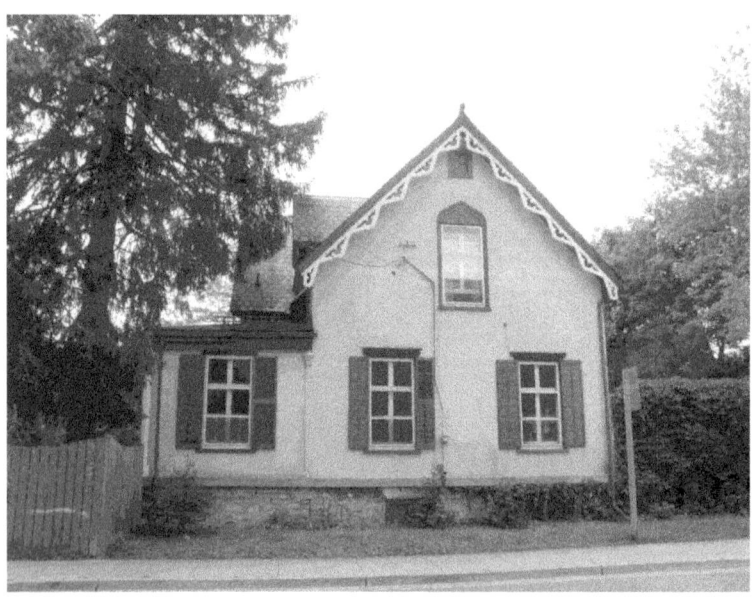

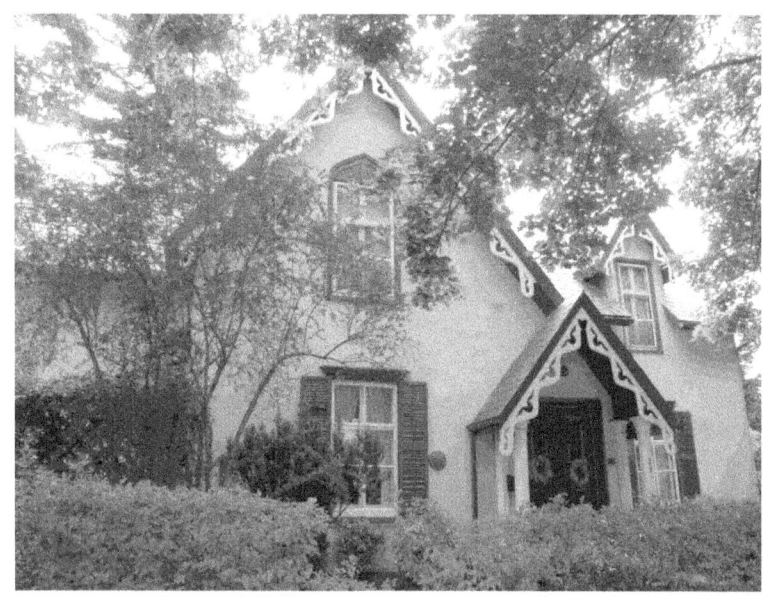

Circa 1850s – intricate vergeboard

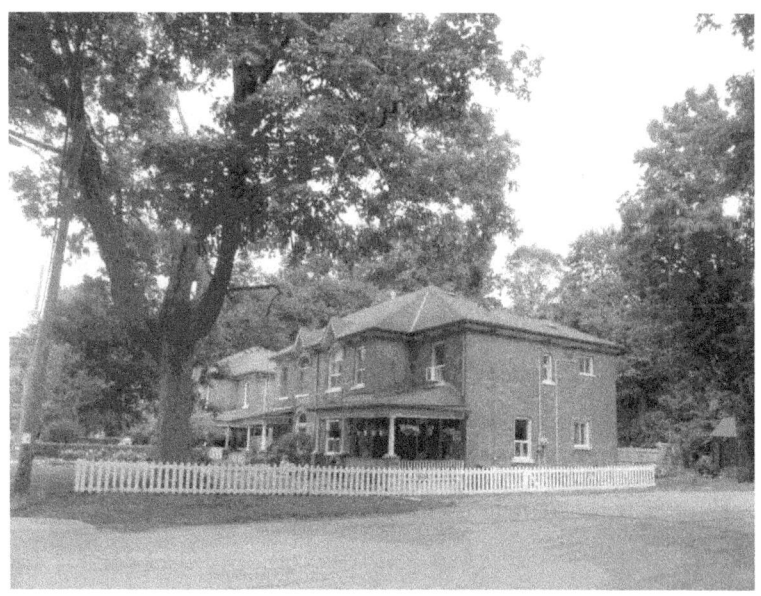

Cross Street

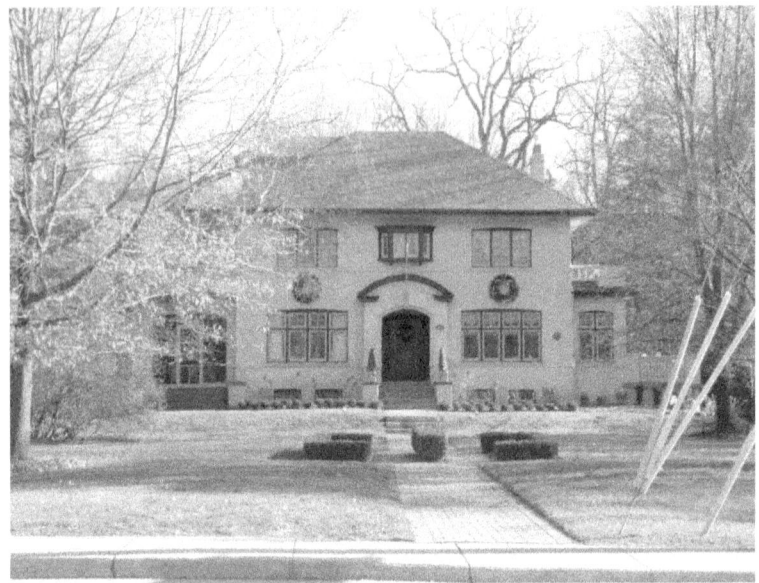

63 Cross Street

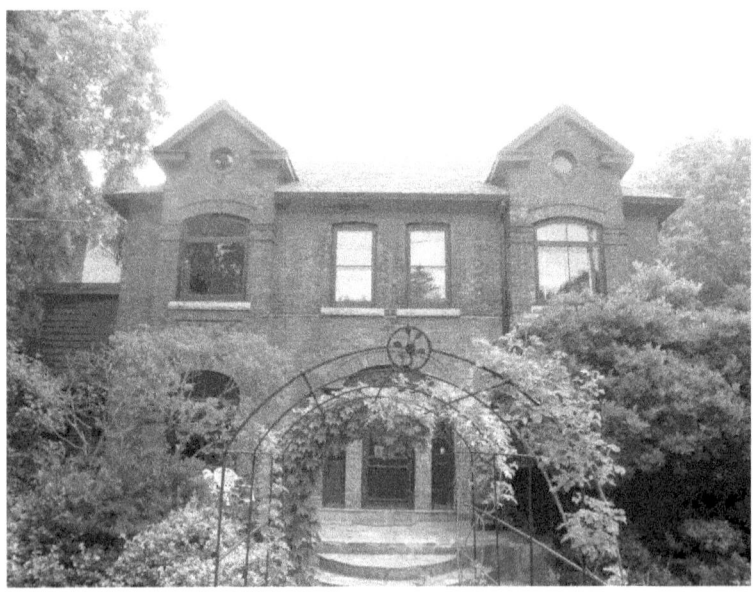

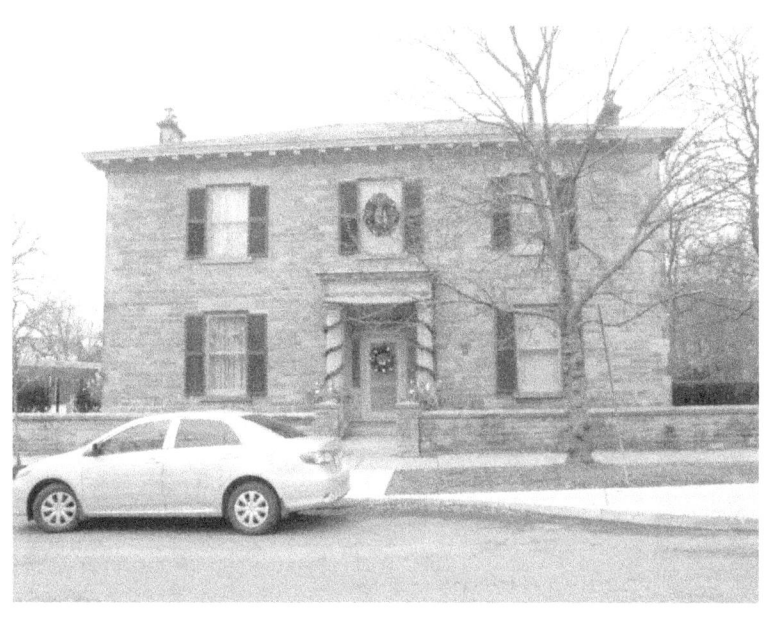

32 Cross Street – circa 1840s

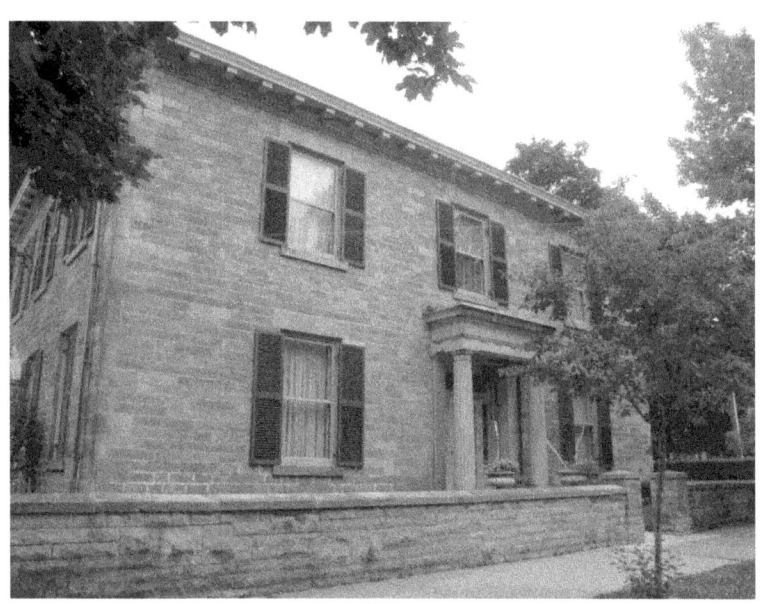

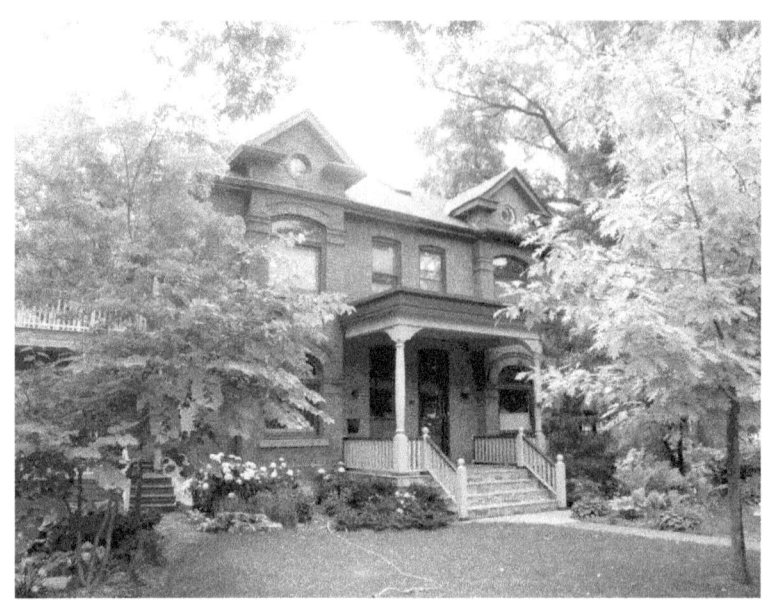

49 Cross Street

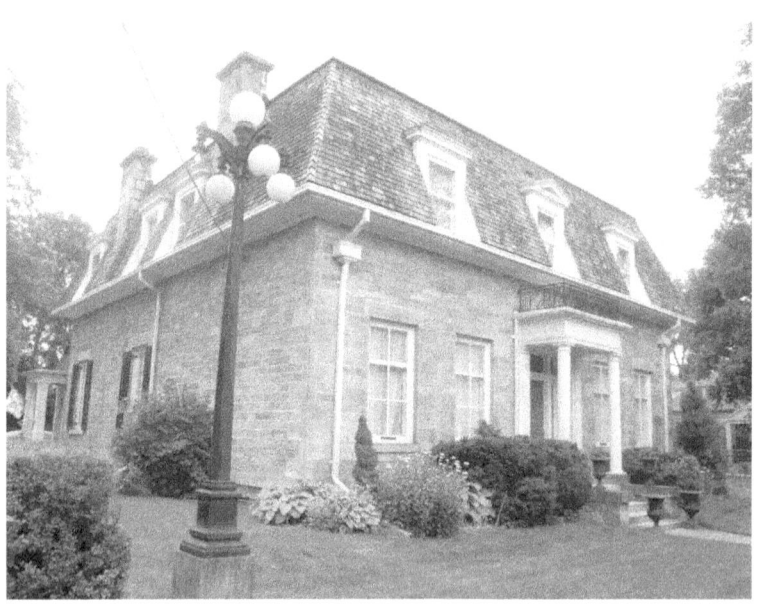

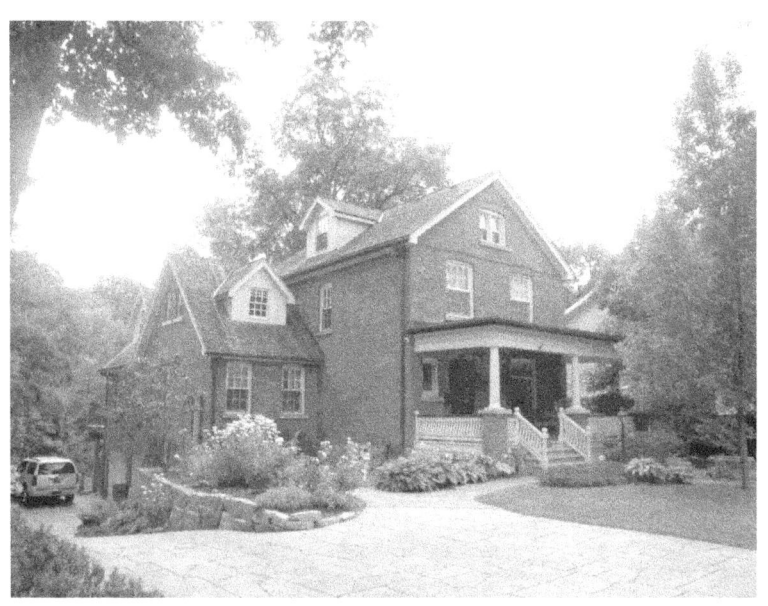

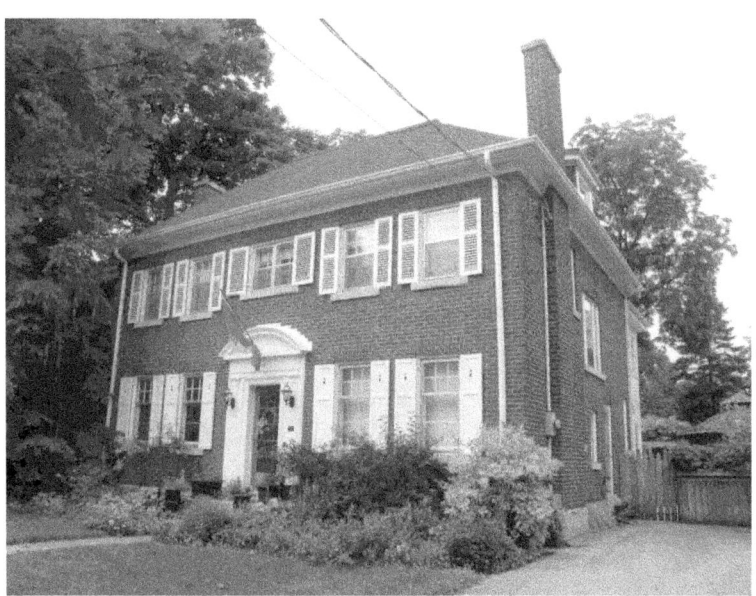

42 Cross Street – Georgian style architecture

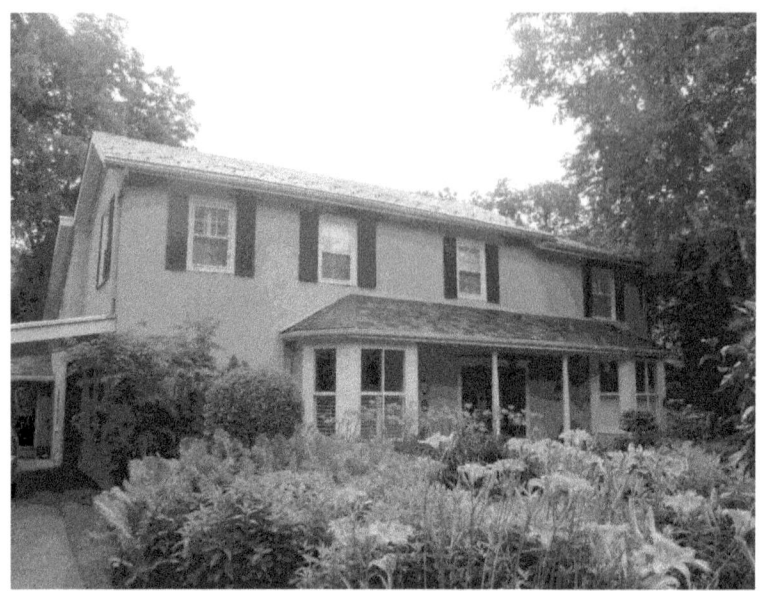

Circa 1830s

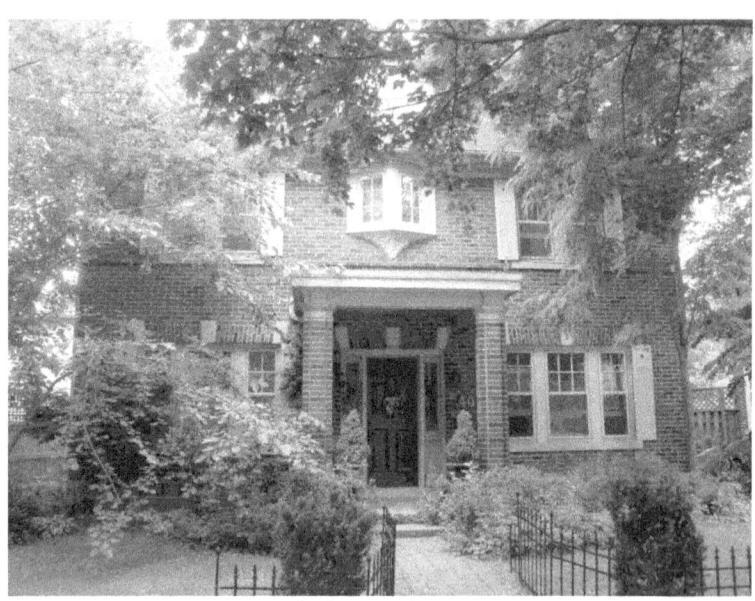

40 Cross Street

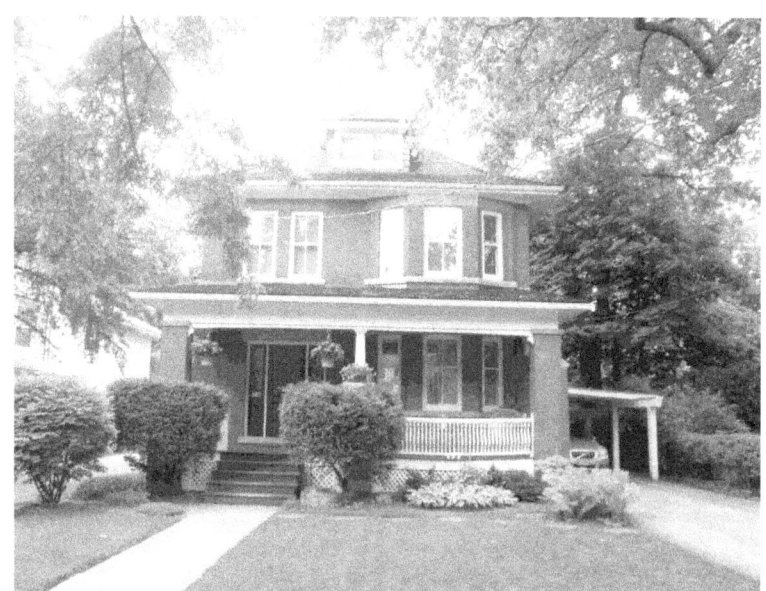

39 Cross Street

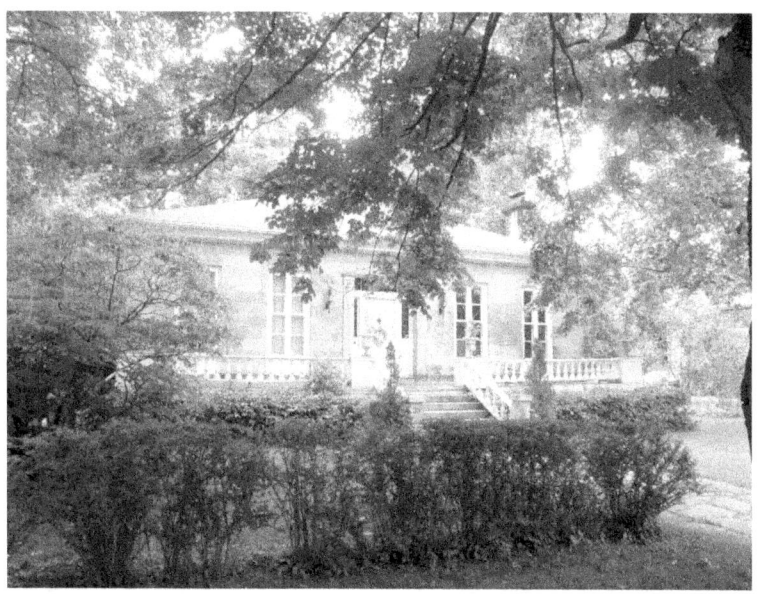

35 Cross Street – circa 1840s

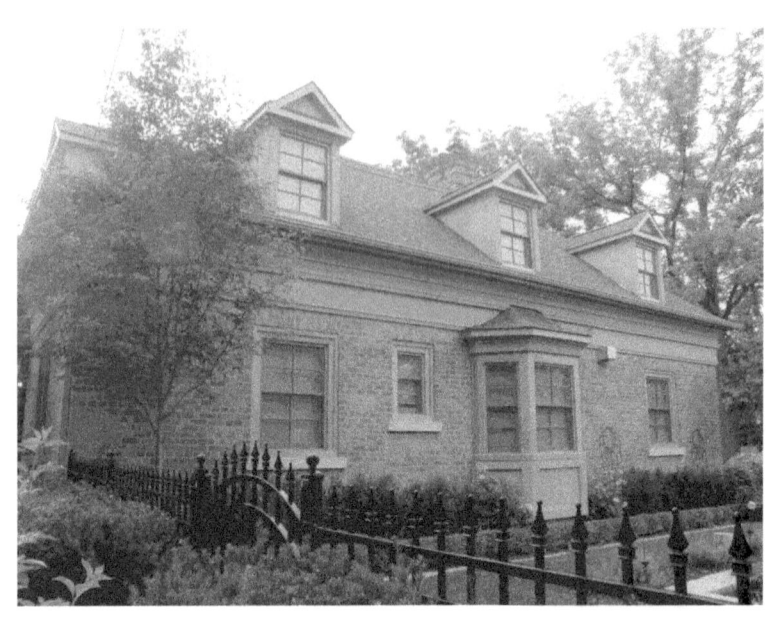

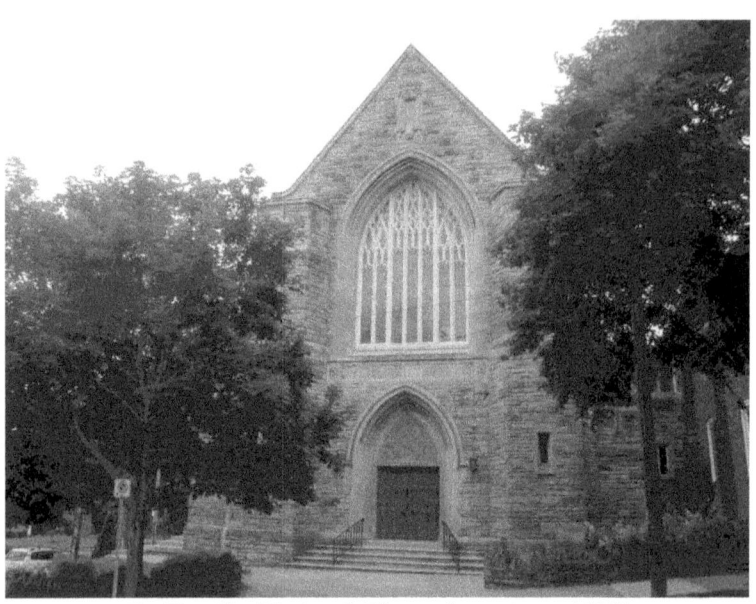

St. Paul's United Church – circa 1855

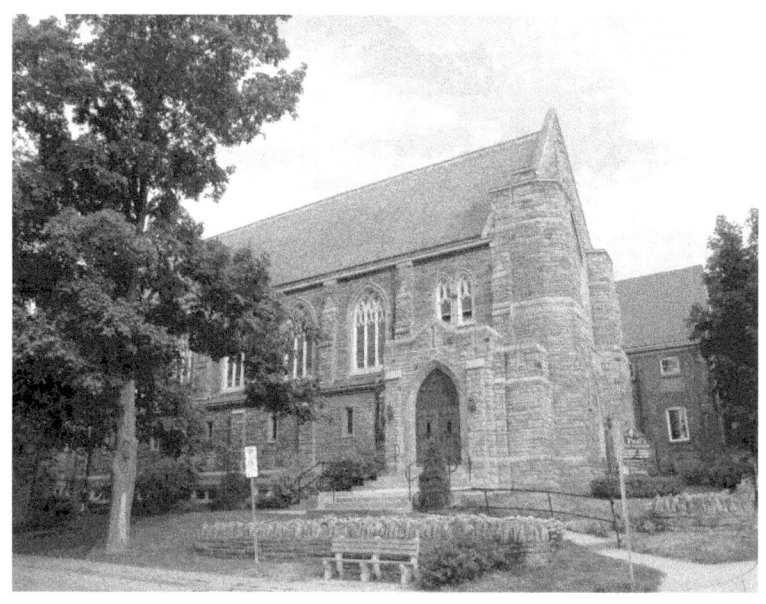

St. Paul's United Church, corner of Cross and Park Streets

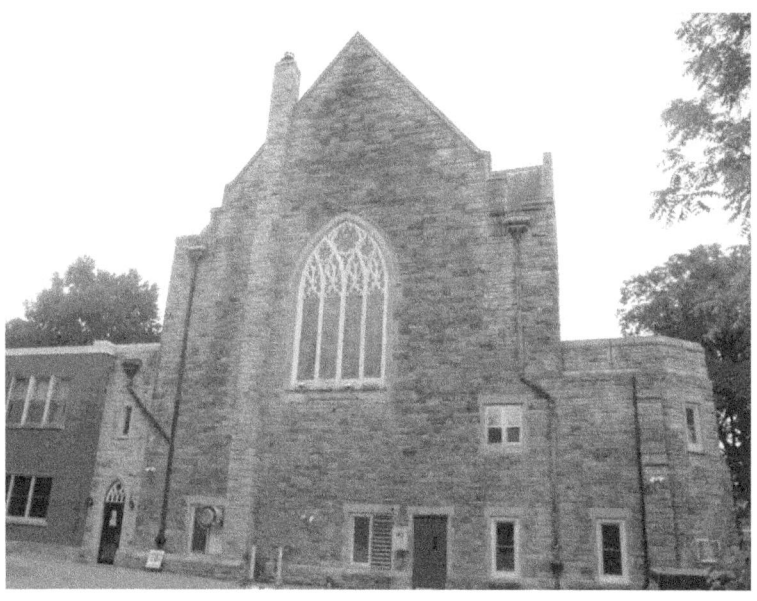

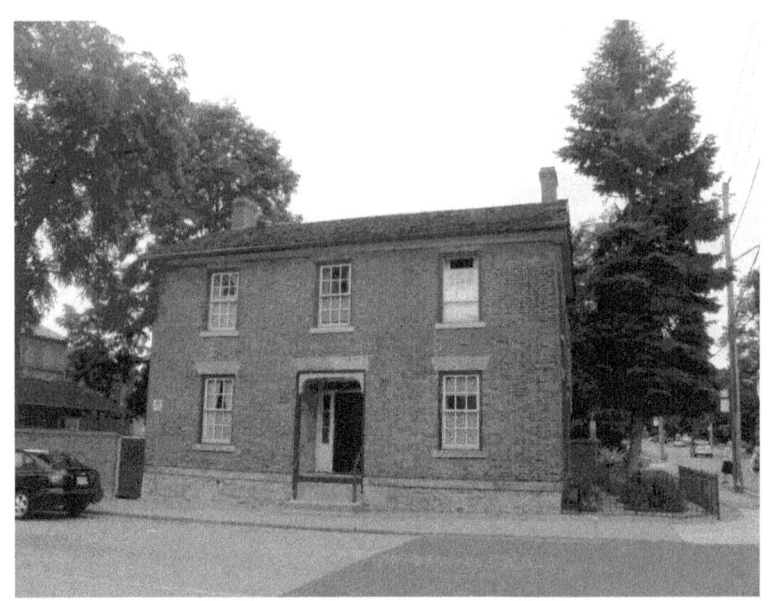

22 Cross Street – circa 1840s

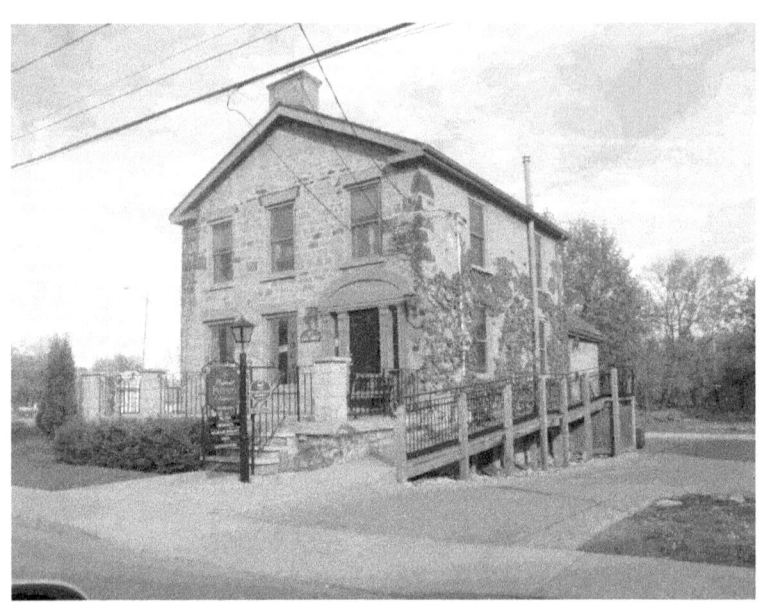

30 York Street - circa 1830s

Melville Street

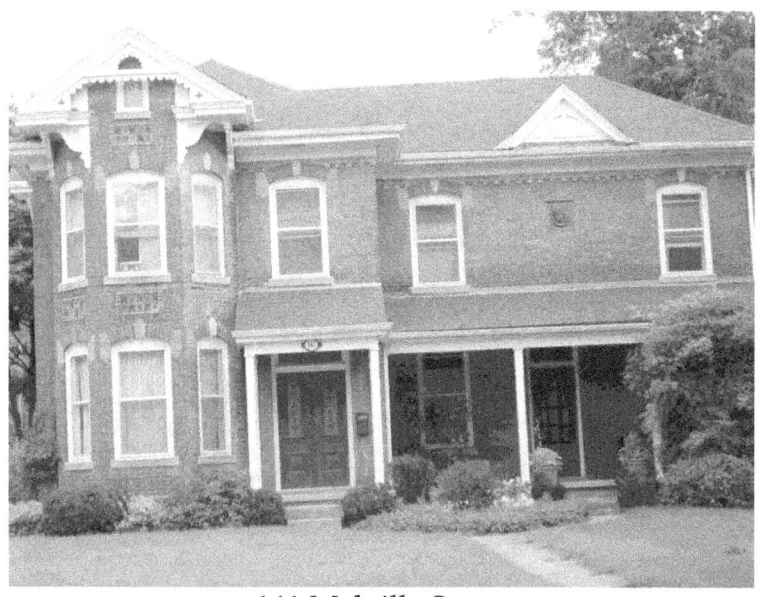

141 Melville Street

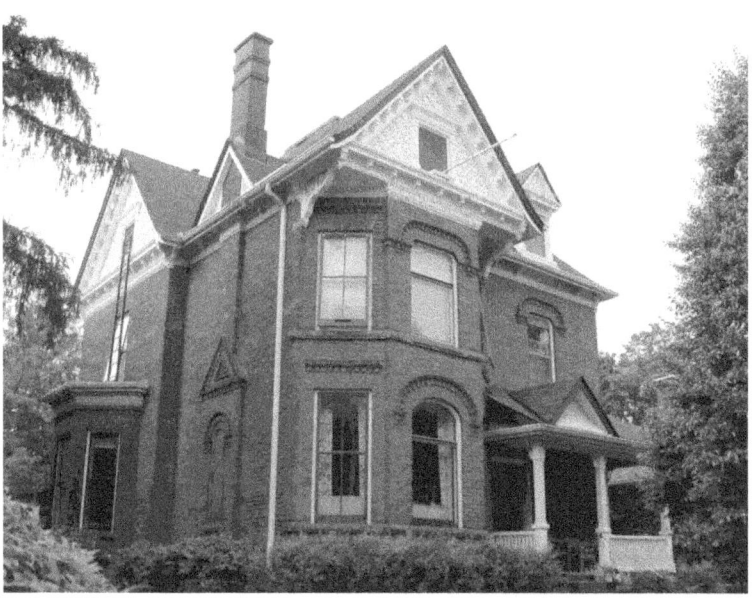

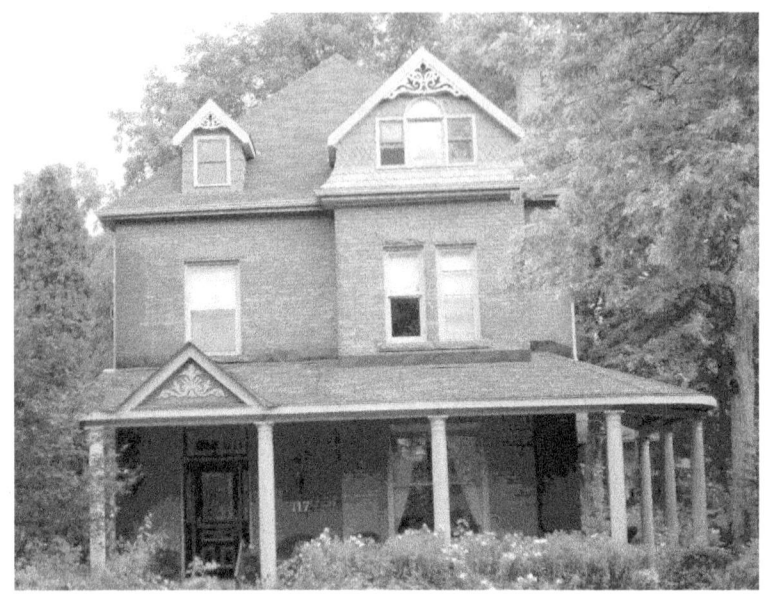

117 Melville Street

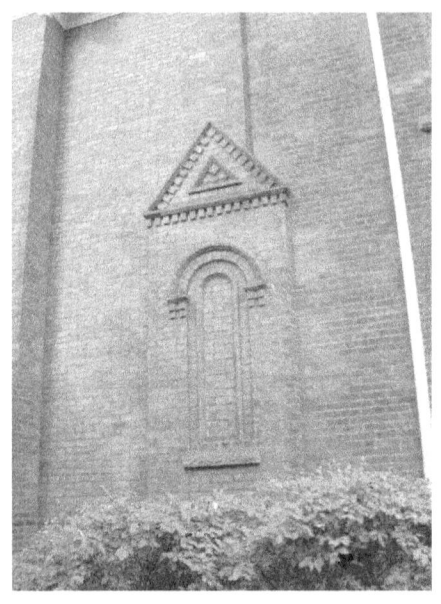

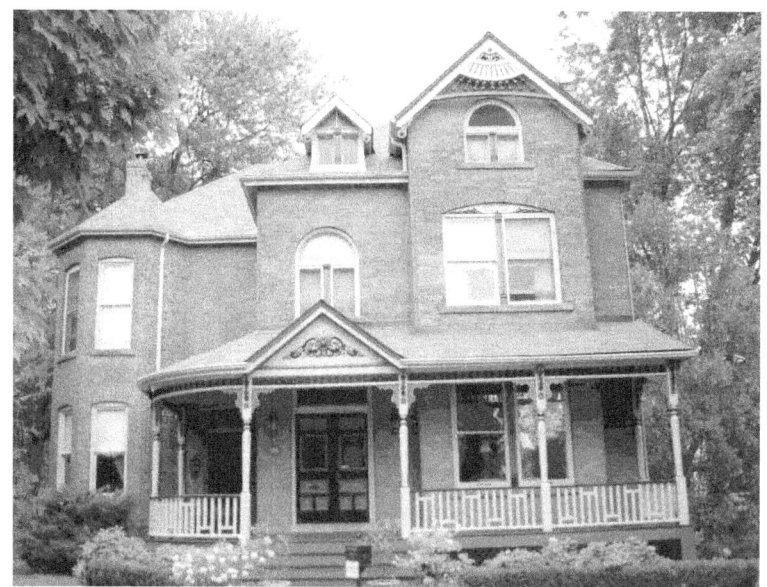

113 Melville Street

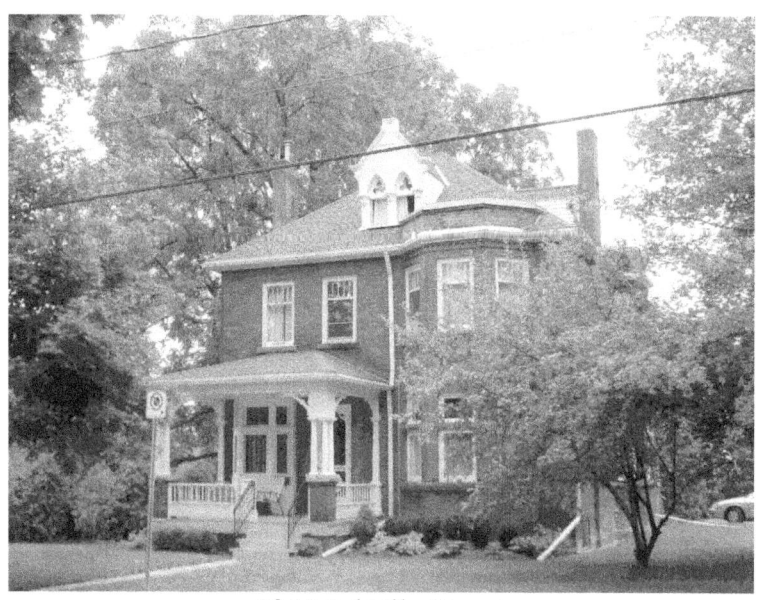

106 Melville Street

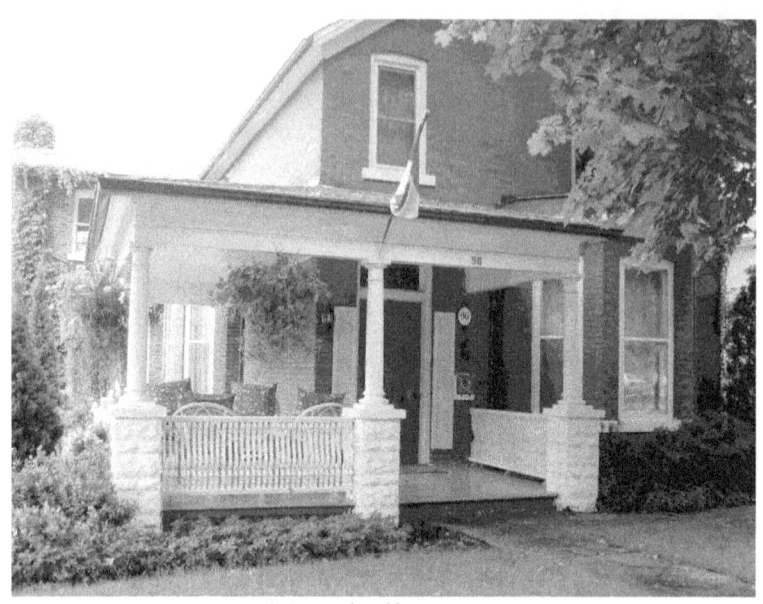

96 Melville Street

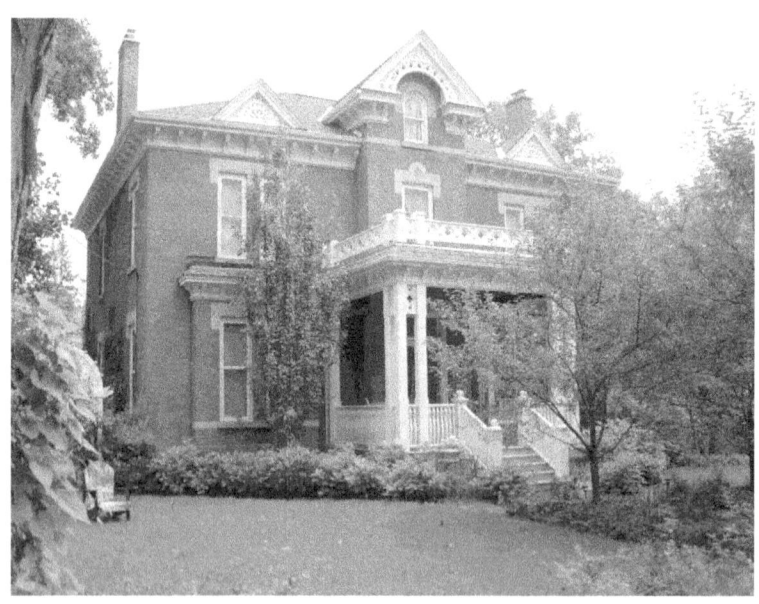

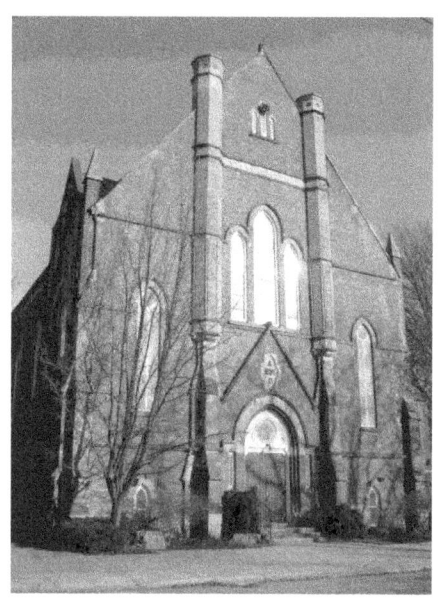

Knox Presbyterian Church – A.D. 1874
Melville Street

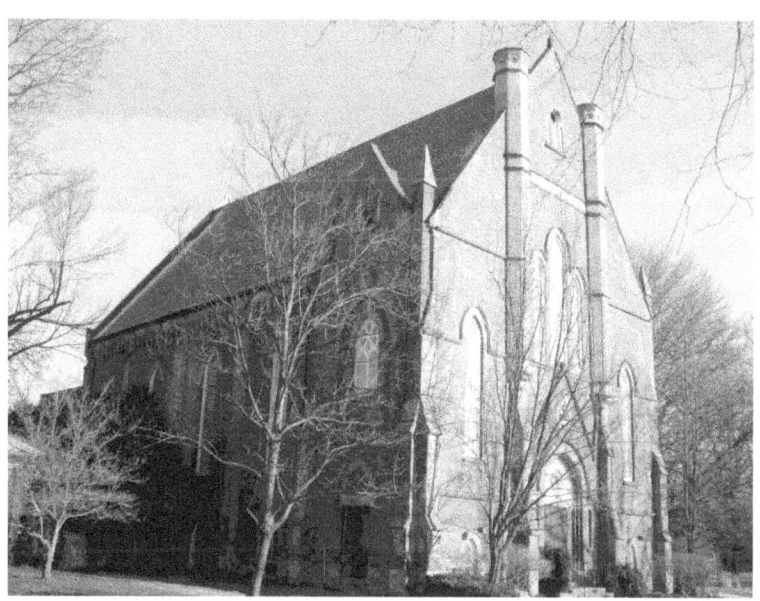

Victoria Street

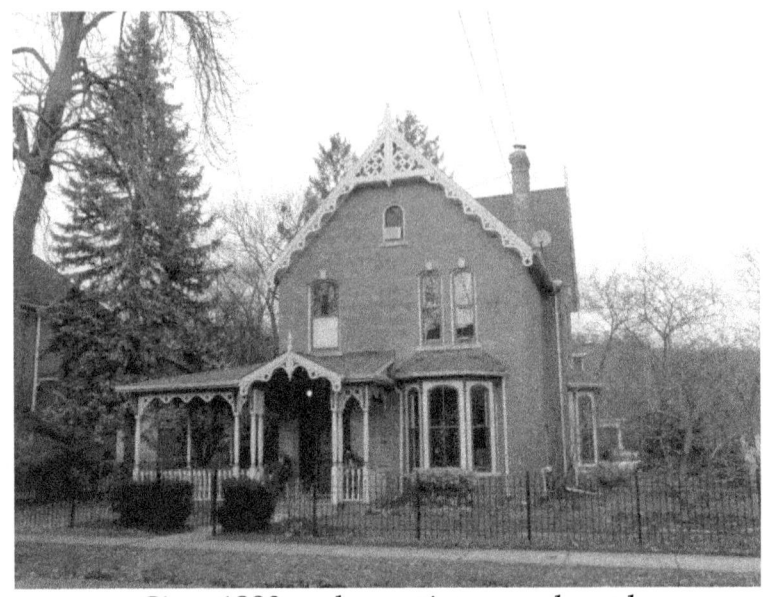

Circa 1880s – decorative vergeboard

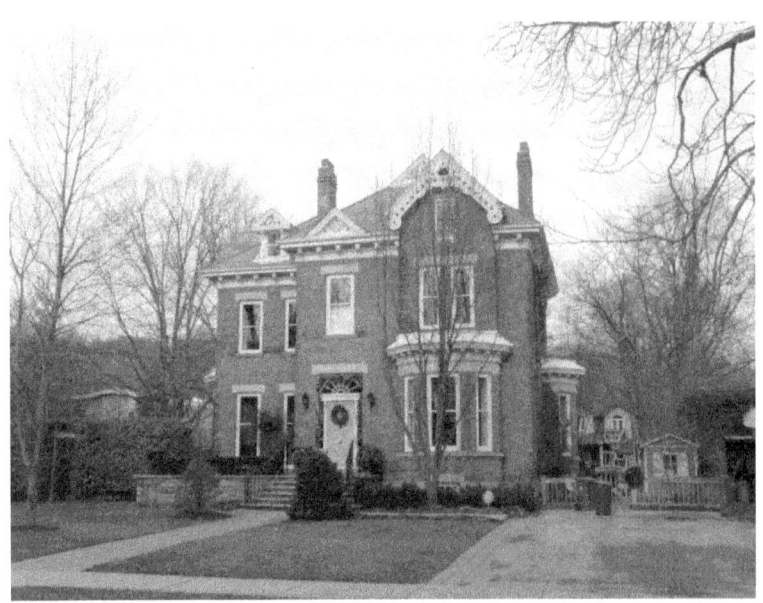

25 Victoria Street

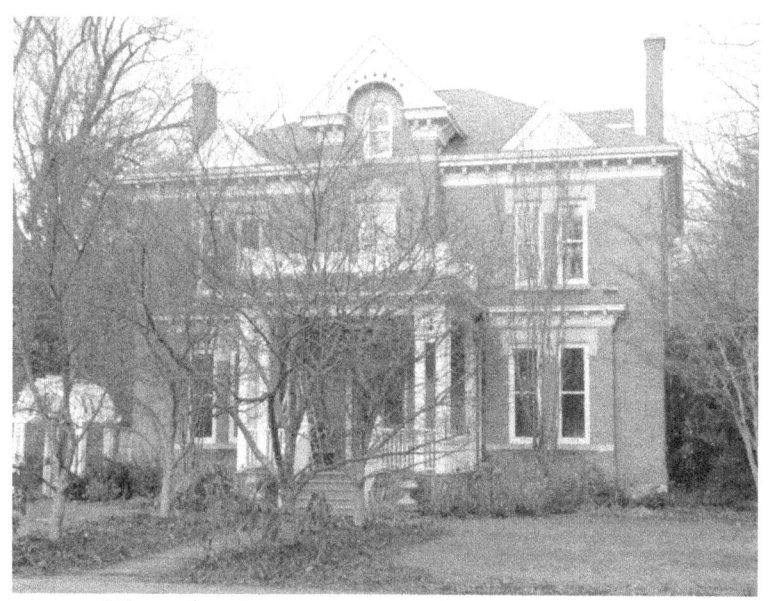

Note the decoration on the Gothic arches

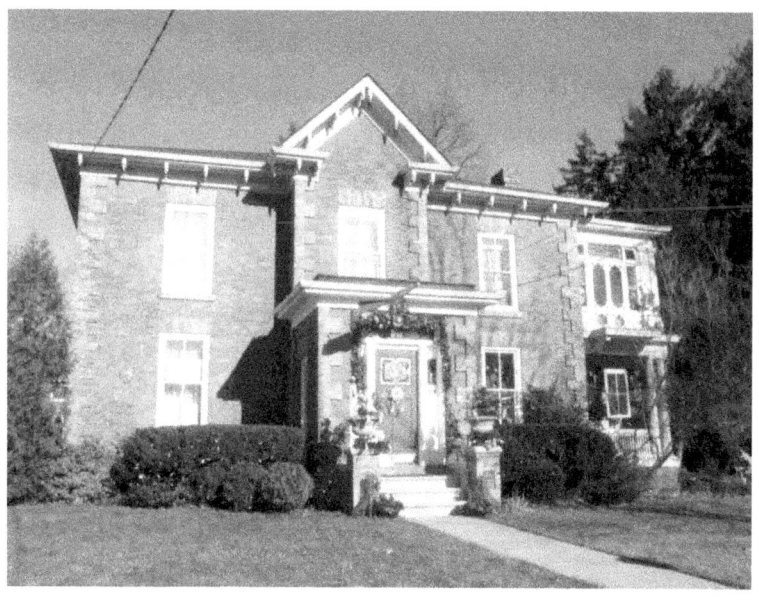

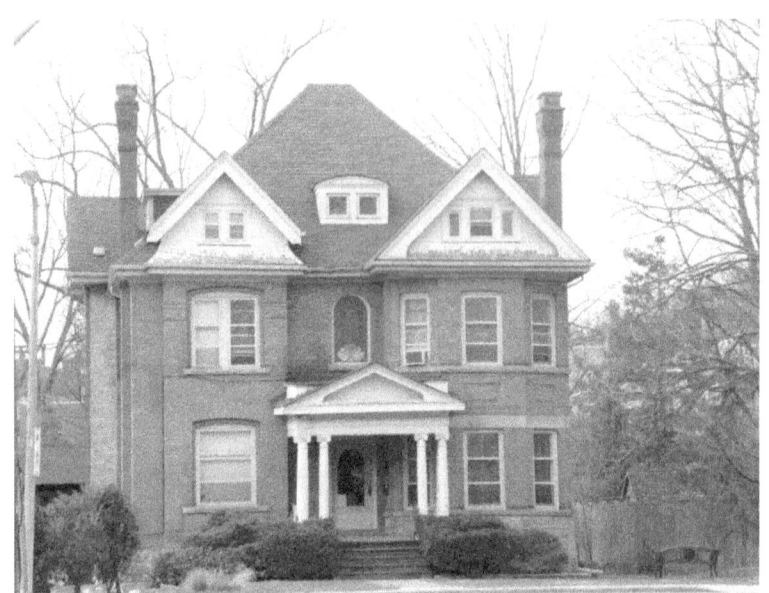

Gothic arches

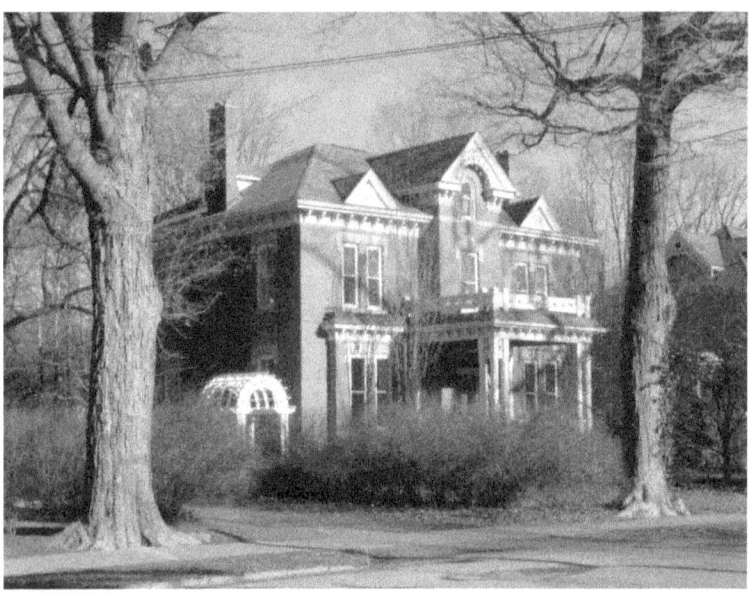

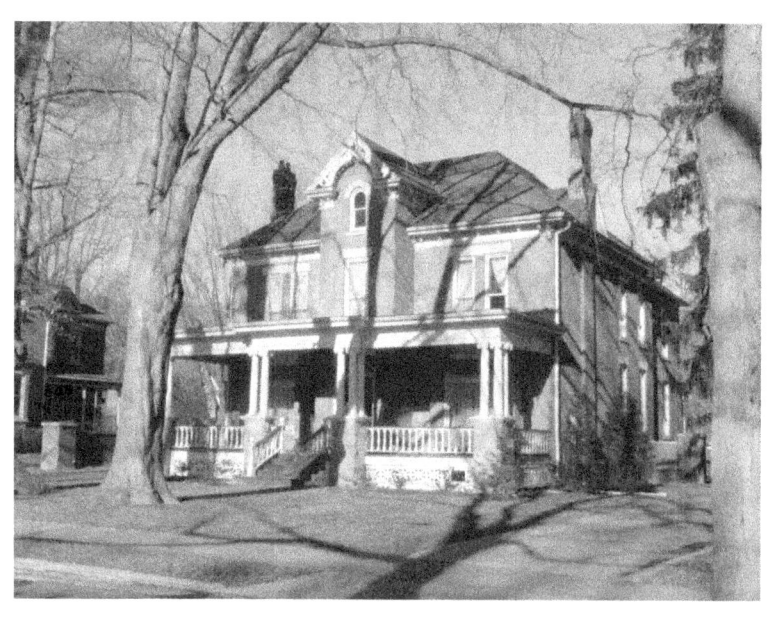

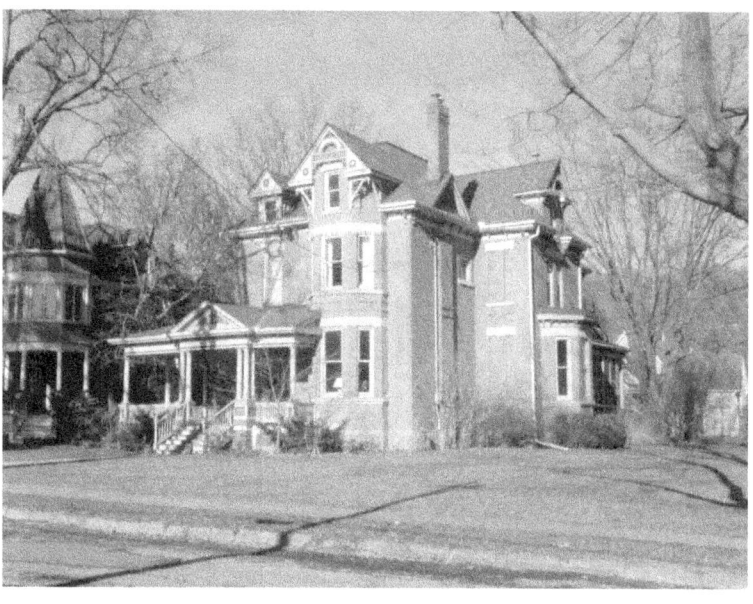

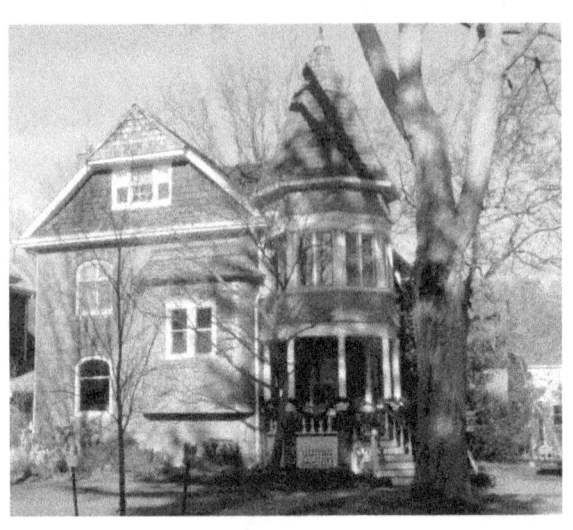

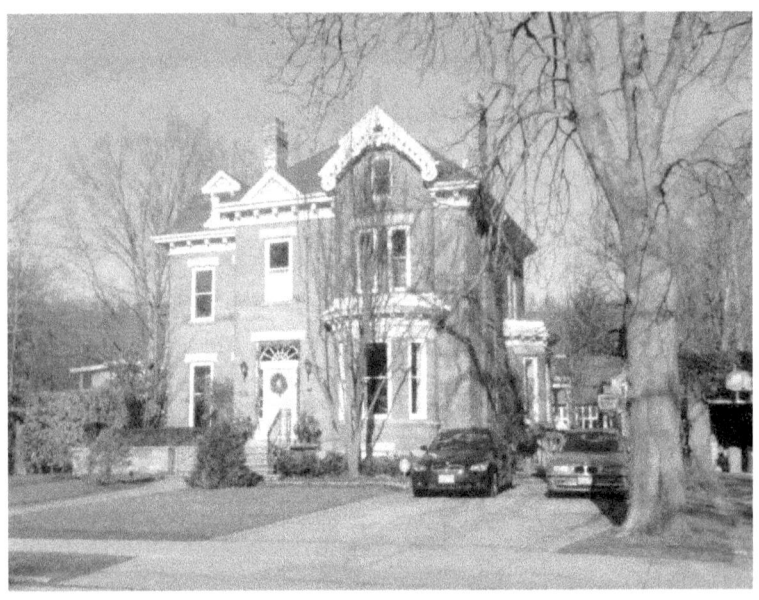

Sydenham Street

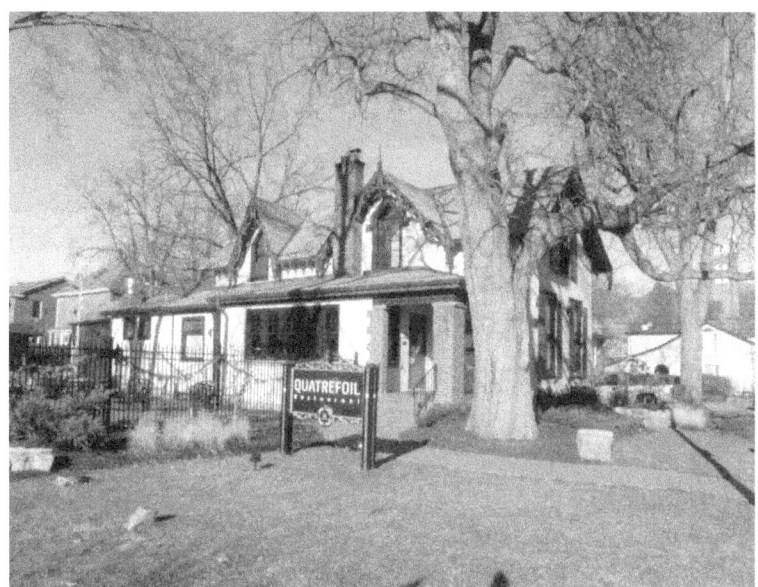

Quatrefoil Restaurant

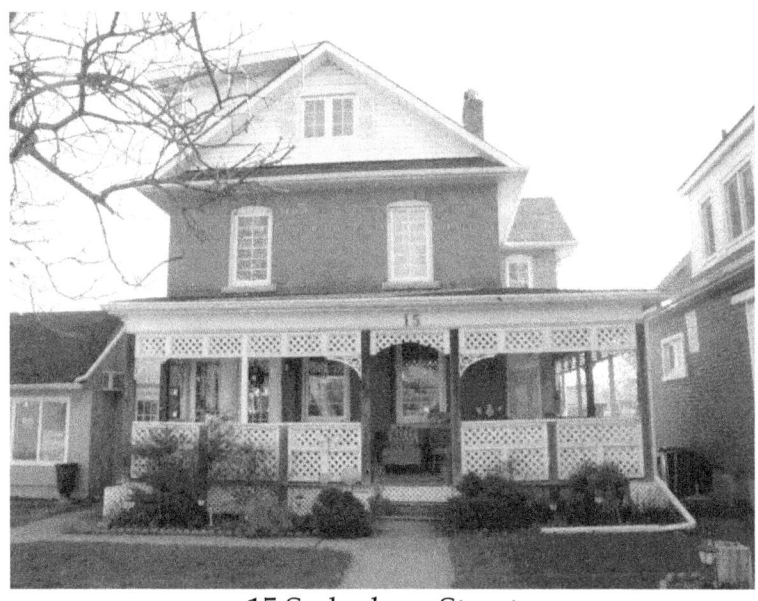

15 Sydenham Street

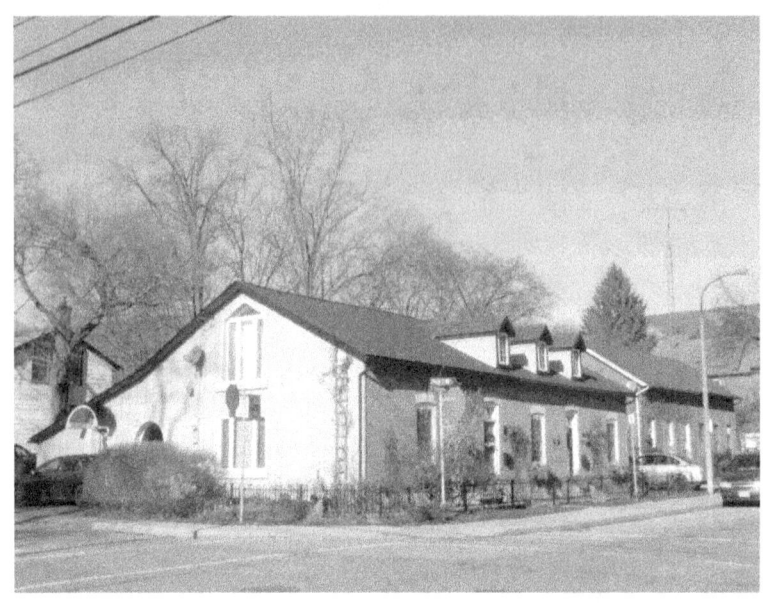

Blacksmith Cottage circa 1859

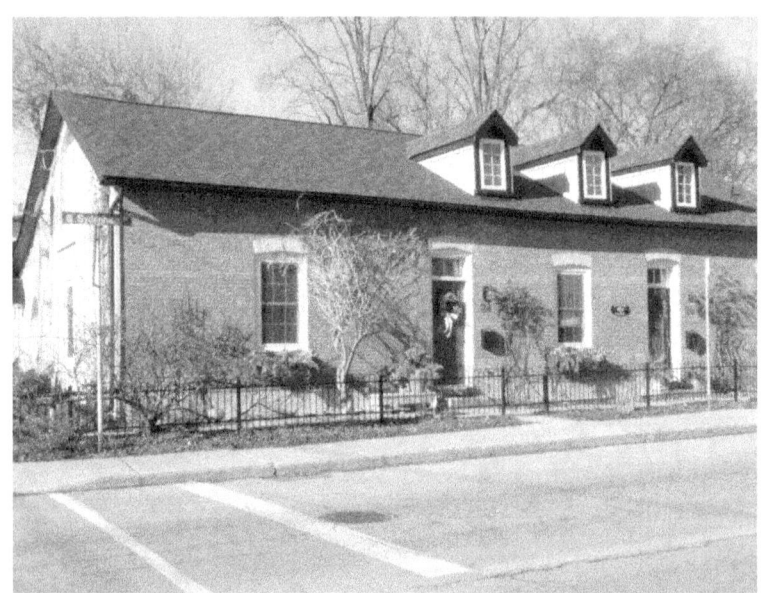

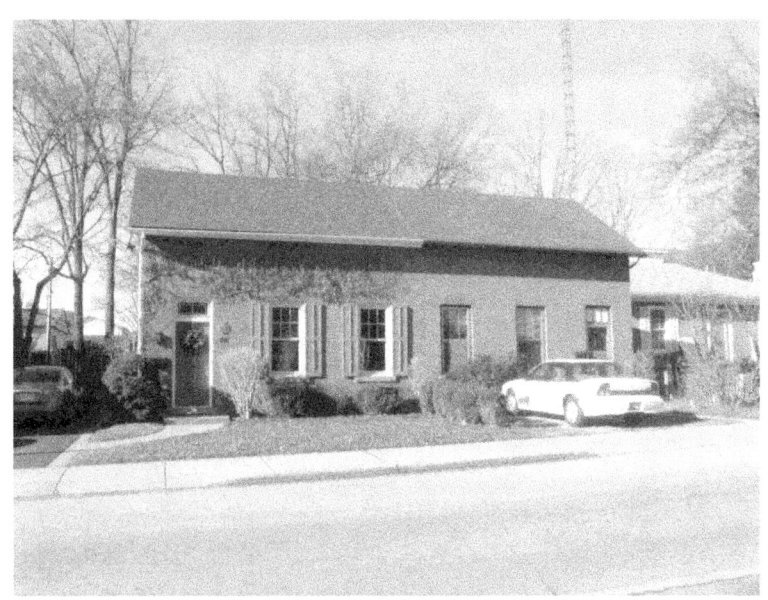

30 Sydenham Street – circa 1870s

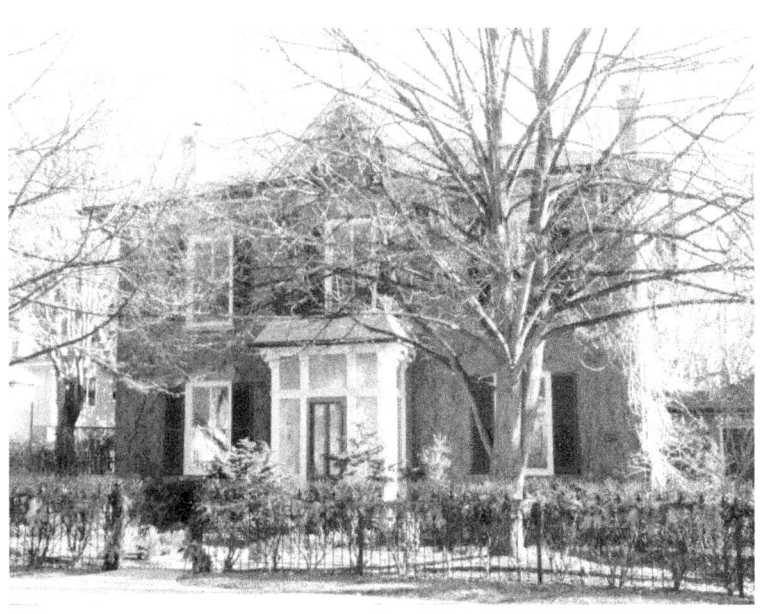

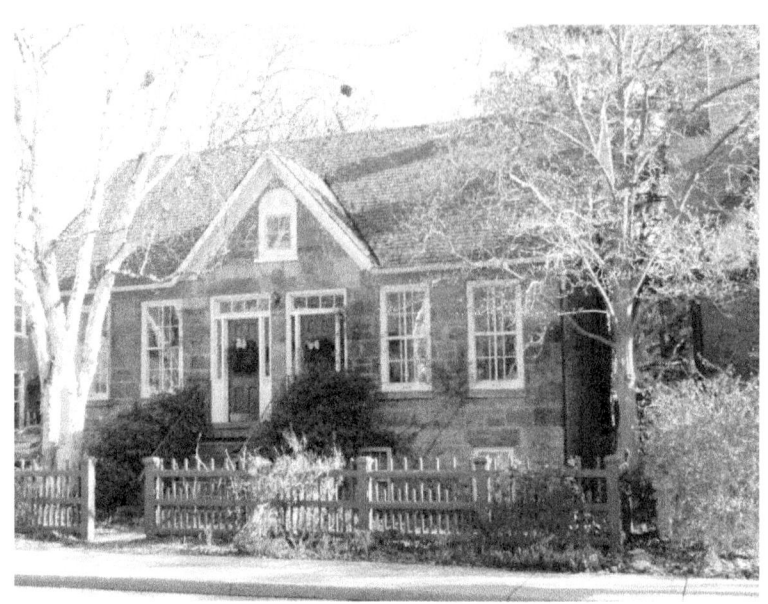

27 Sydenham Street – circa 1850s

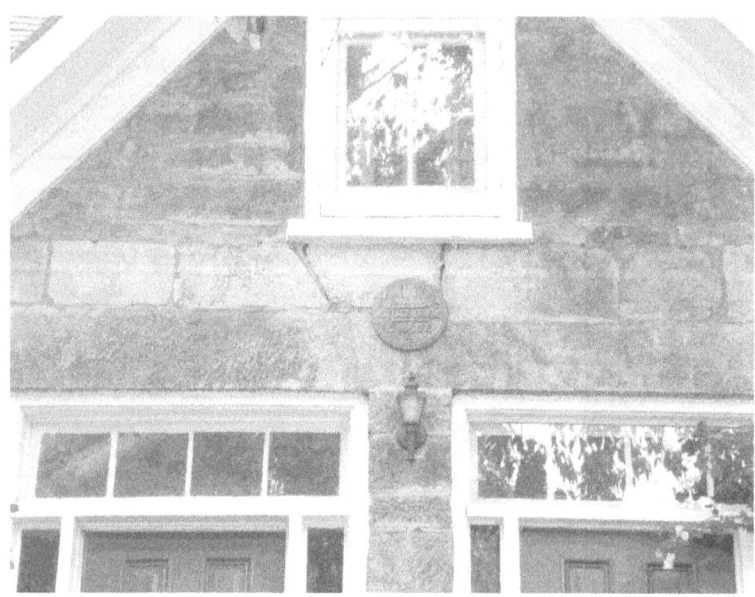

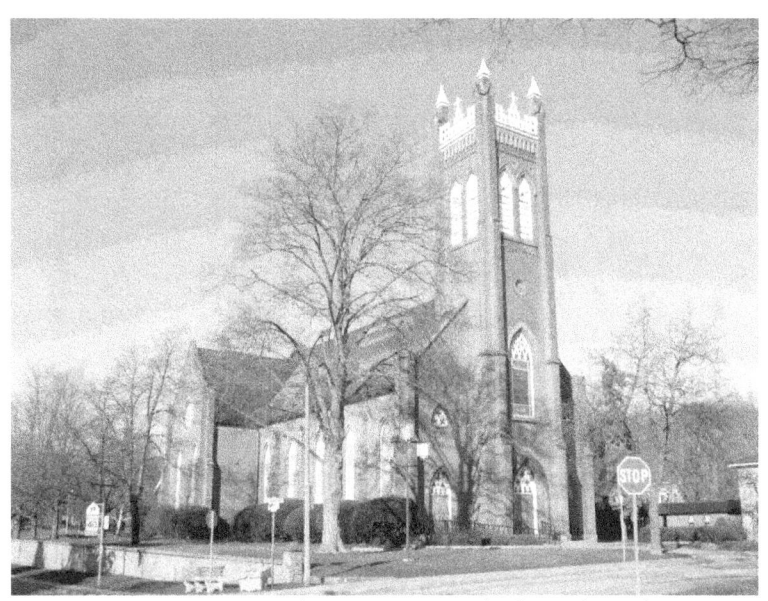

St. Augustine's Roman Catholic Church
Sydenham Street

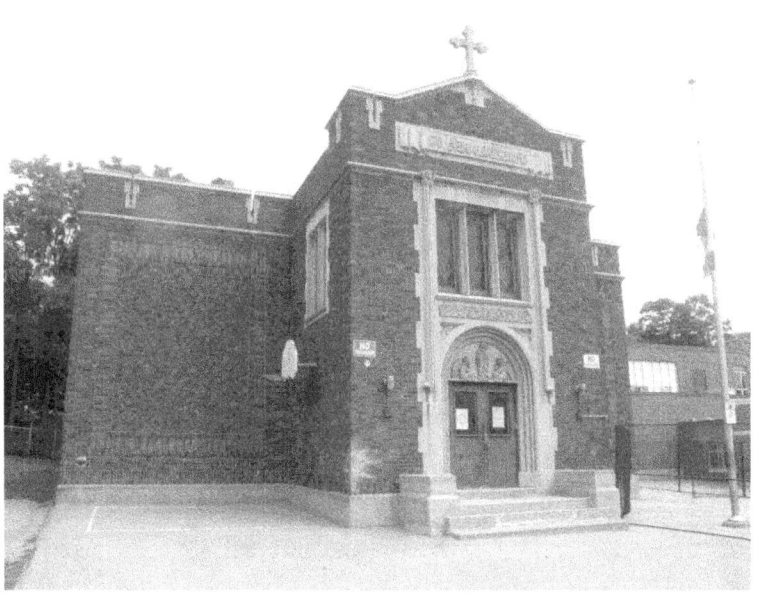

St. Augustine's School

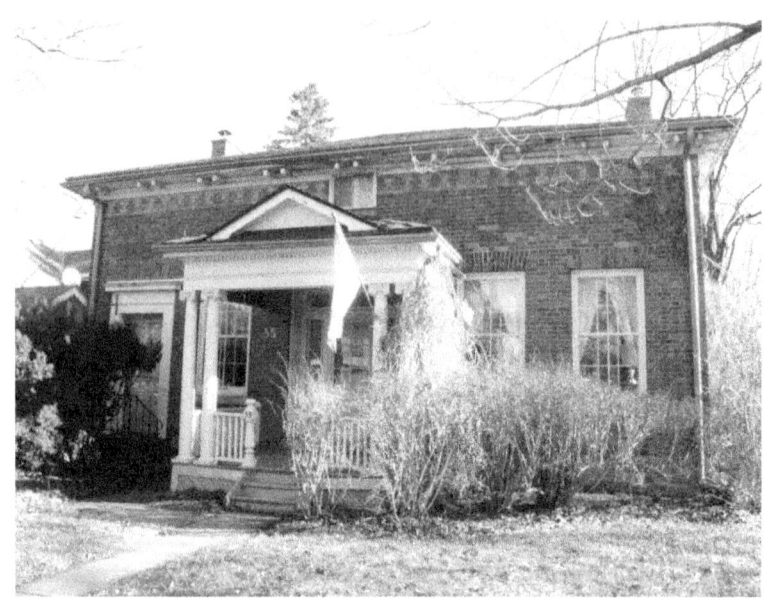

55 Sydenham Street

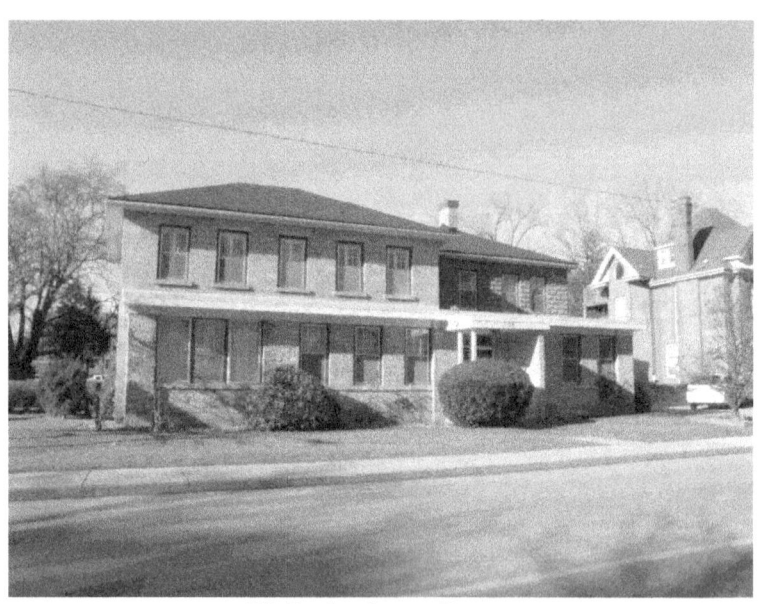

58 Sydenham Street

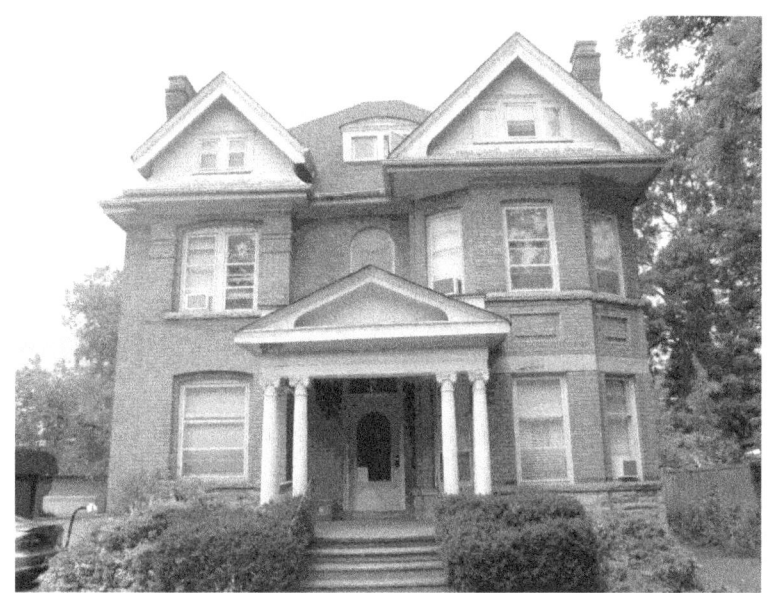

60 Sydenham Street

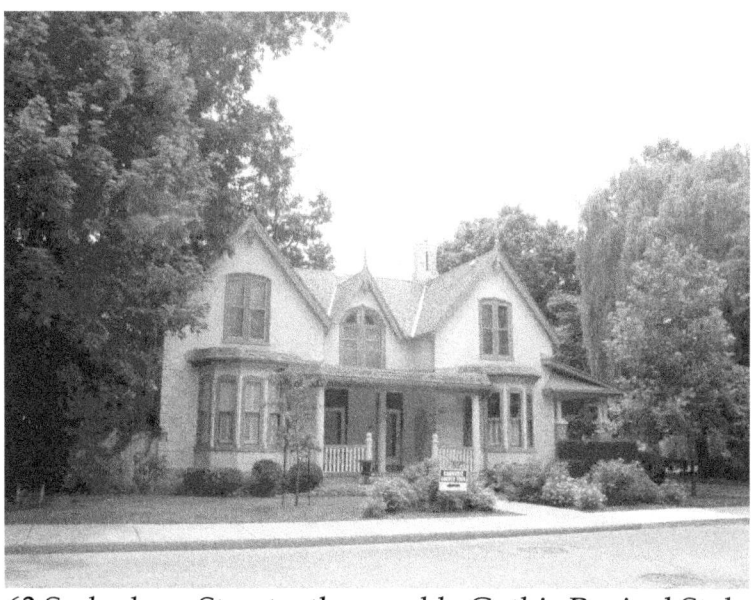

63 Sydenham Street – three gable Gothic Revival Style

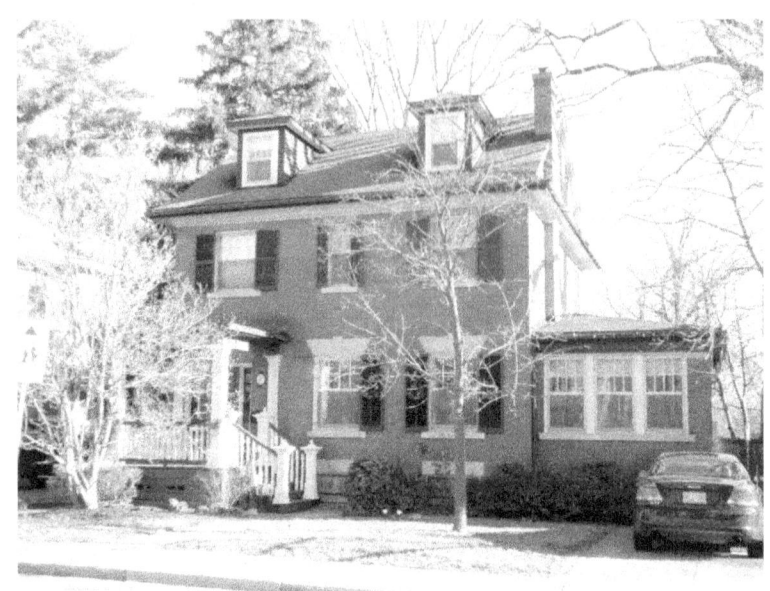

67 Sydenham Street

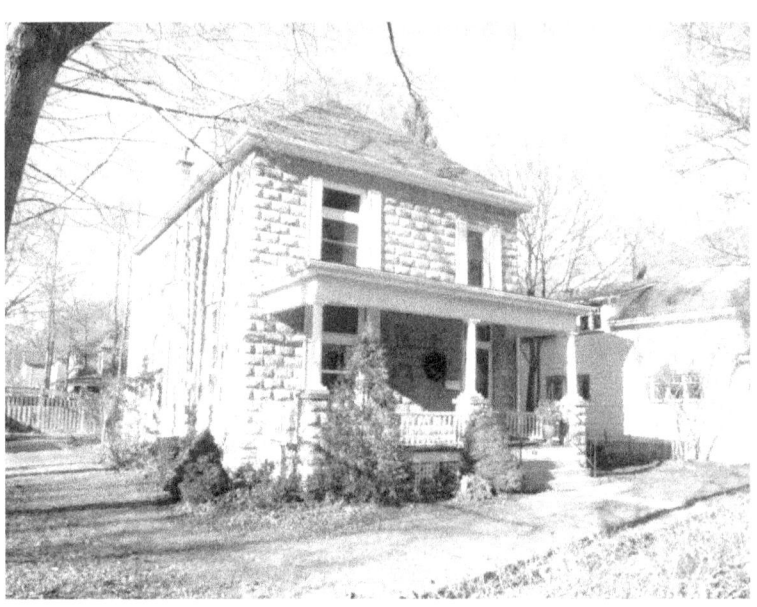

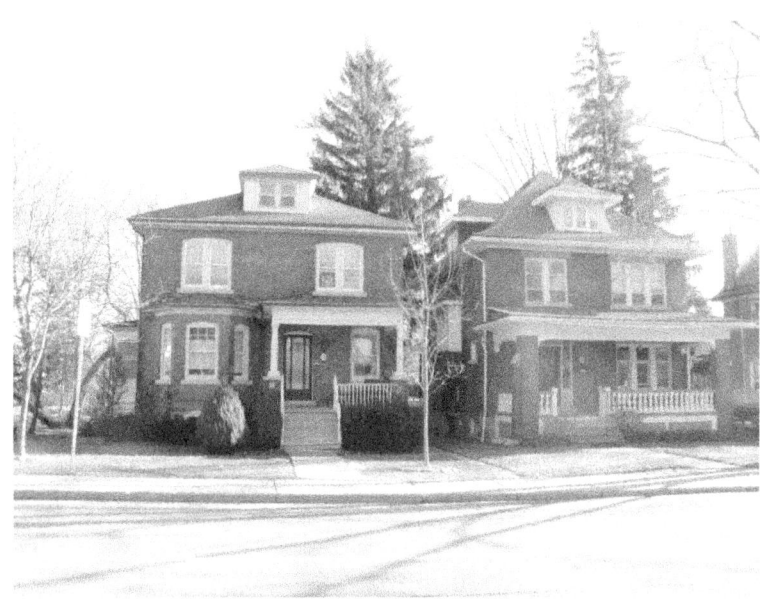

71 and 73 Sydenham Street

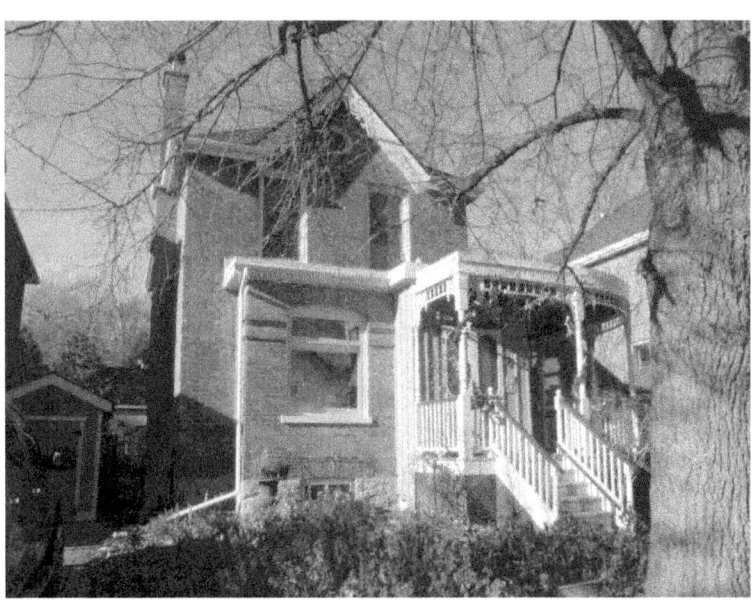

72 Sydenham Street

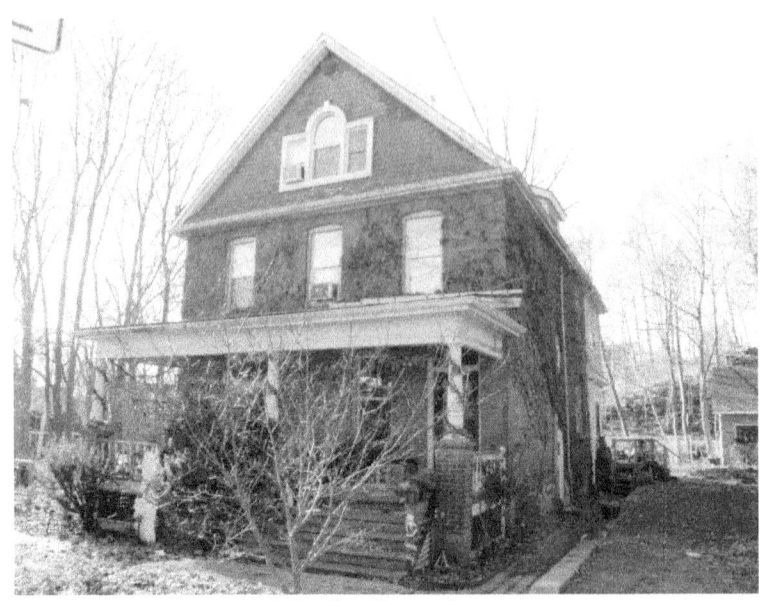

82 Sydenham Street

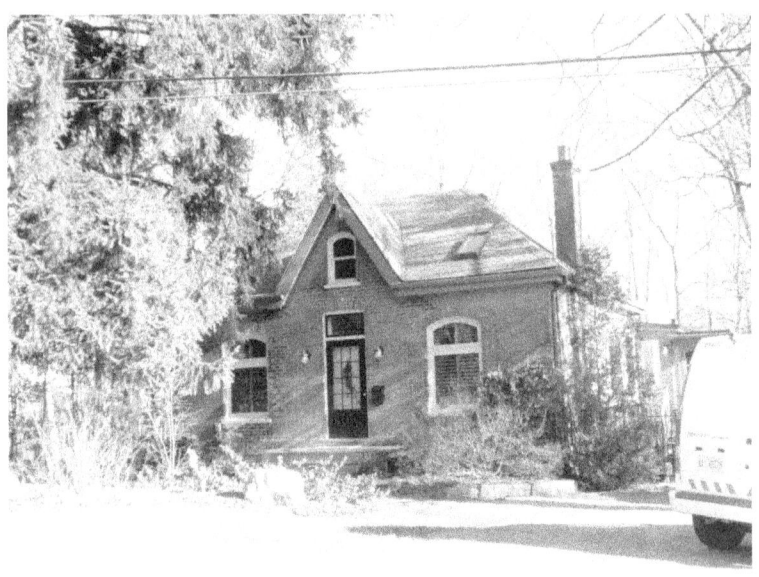

Gothic revival style cottage

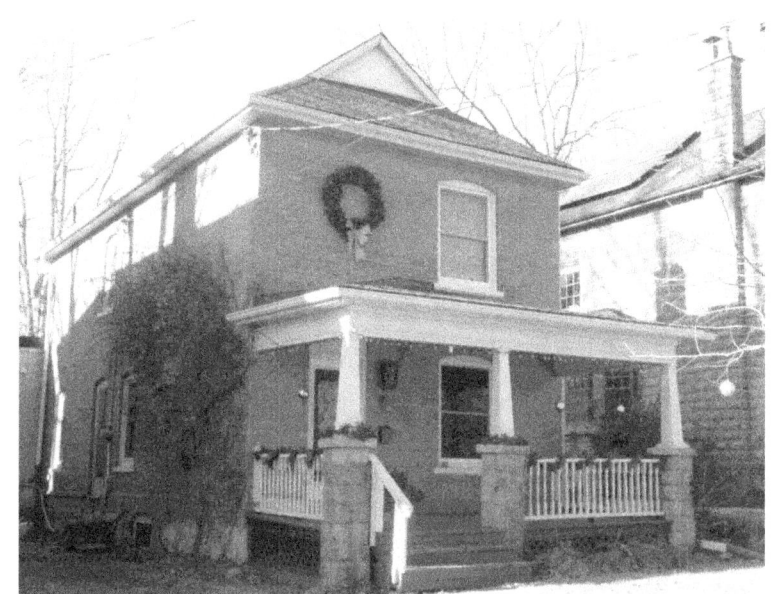

92 Sydenham Street

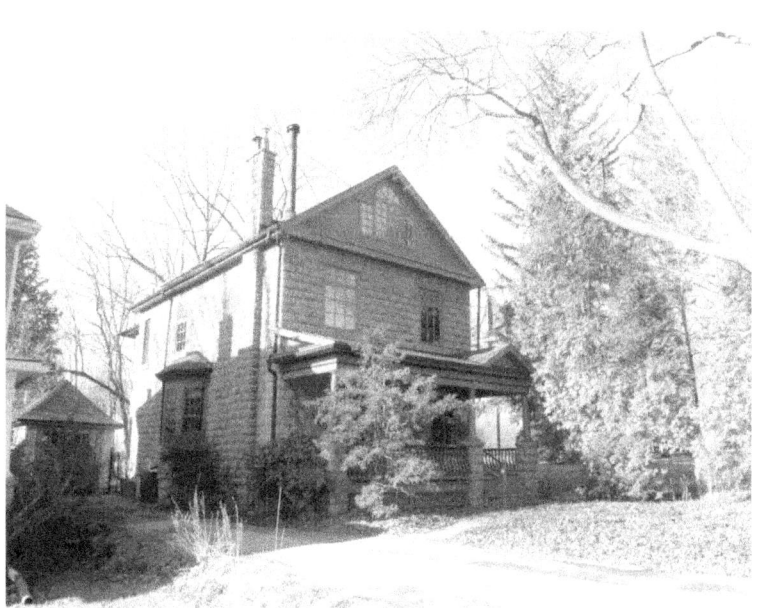

Cement block house – cheaper to construct

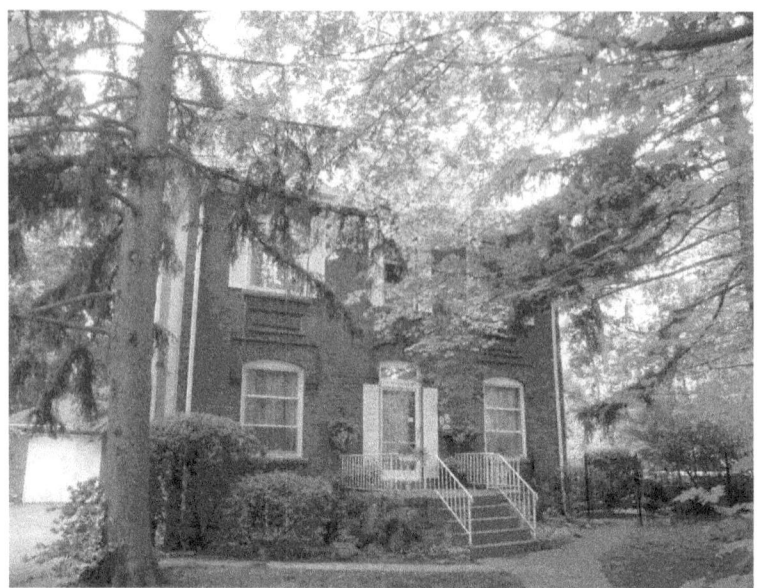

98 Sydenham Street – a beauty hidden among the trees

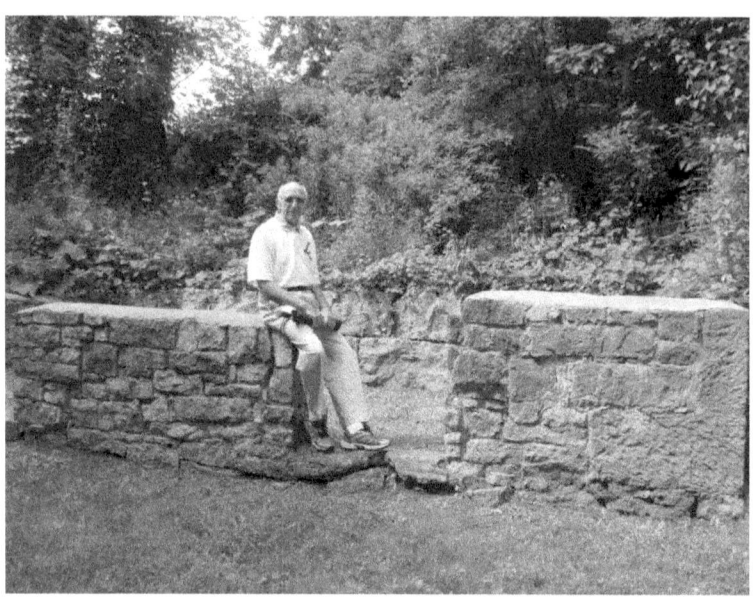

Remnants of an 1840s Mercantile Block at Bullocks Corners consisting of a general store, shoemaker shop, harness shop, flour and feed store, and a public hall

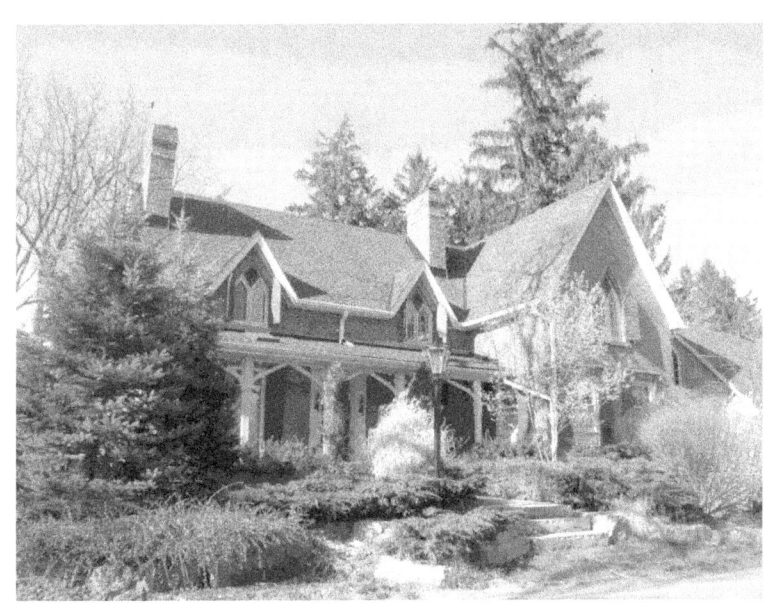

Webster's Fall Road – front view

End view

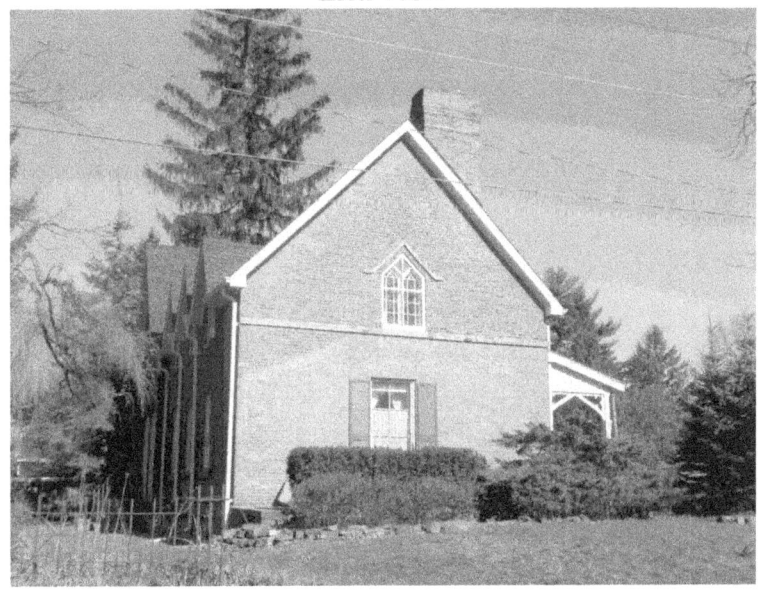

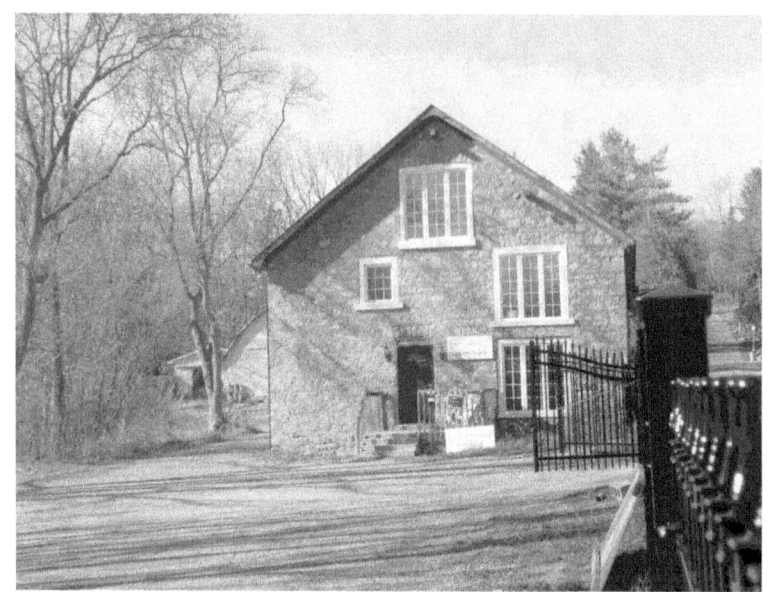

Old stone building on Webster's Falls Road

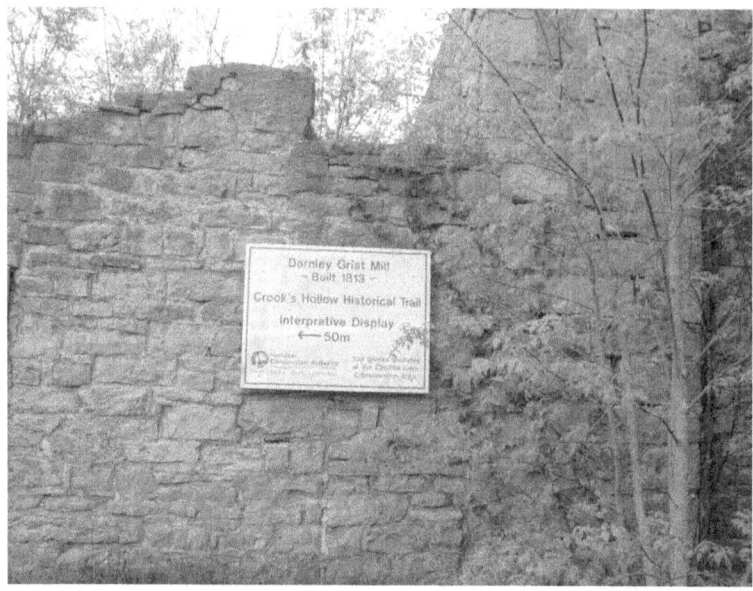

Darnley Grist Mill built 1813 of stone from quarry near Morden's Mills downstream. The building was three stories high with a 9-metre waterwheel mounted on the wall beside Spencer Creek, and had four sets of grindstones.

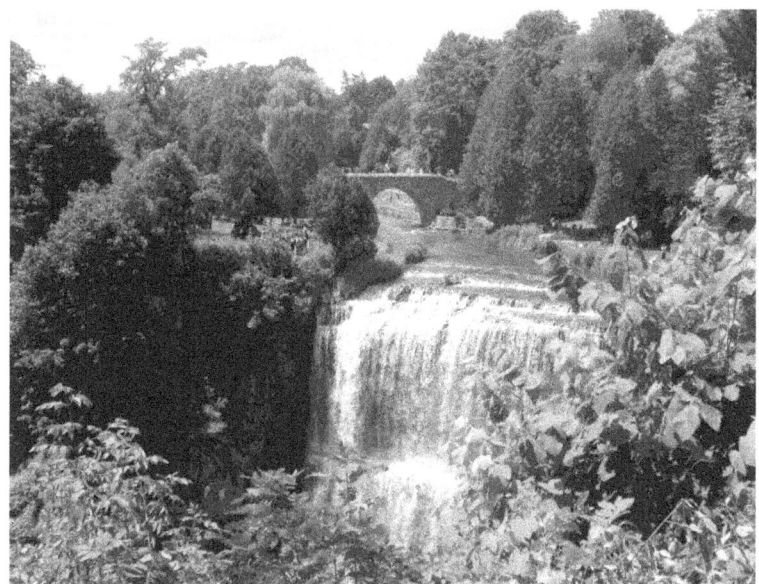

Webster's Falls with cobblestone bridge in background
Our wedding pictures were taken in the park.

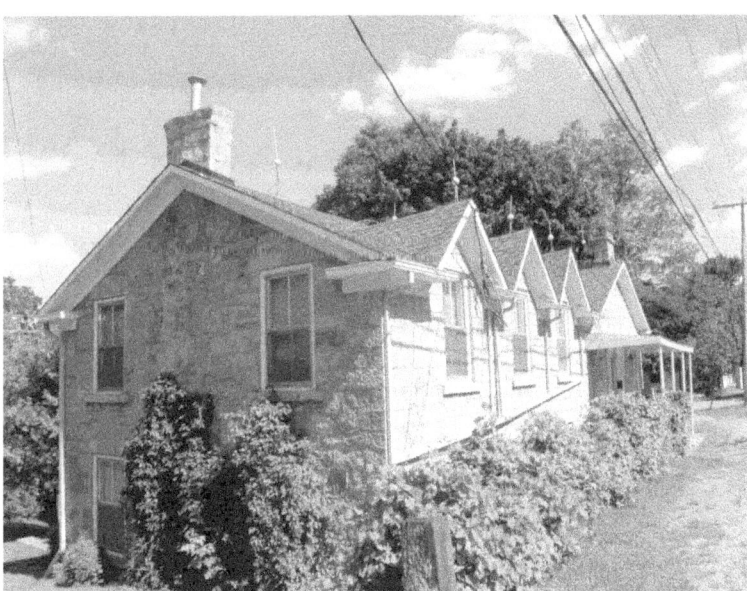

Bullocks Corners limestone house

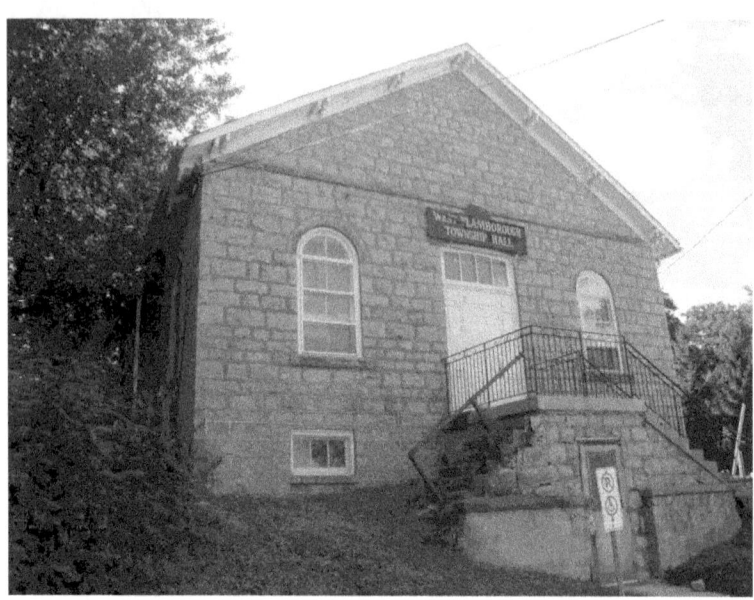

West Flamborough Township Hall
Harry and I were married here on August 13, 1972.

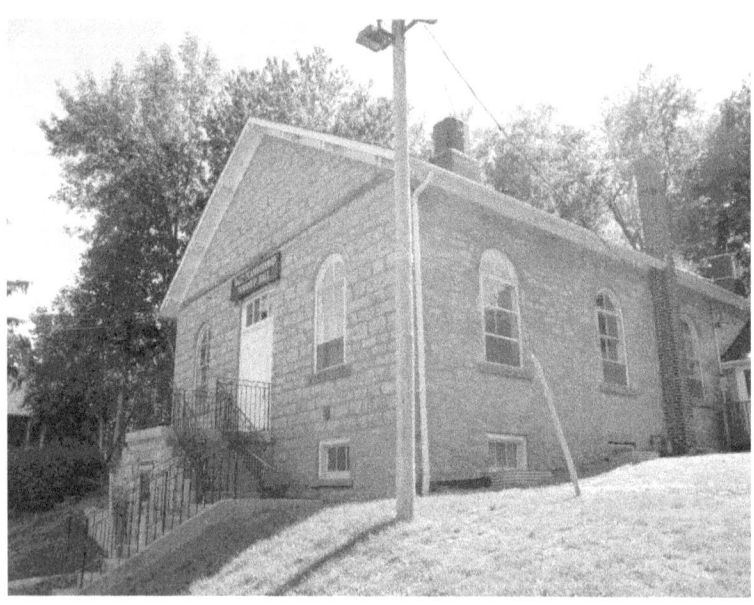

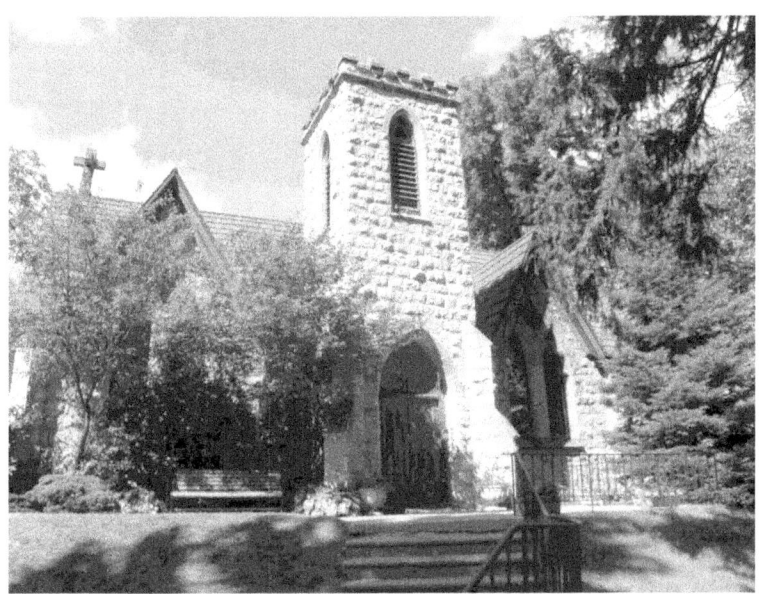

Christ Church – Anglican
Bullocks Corners – built in 1864

Cayley Street

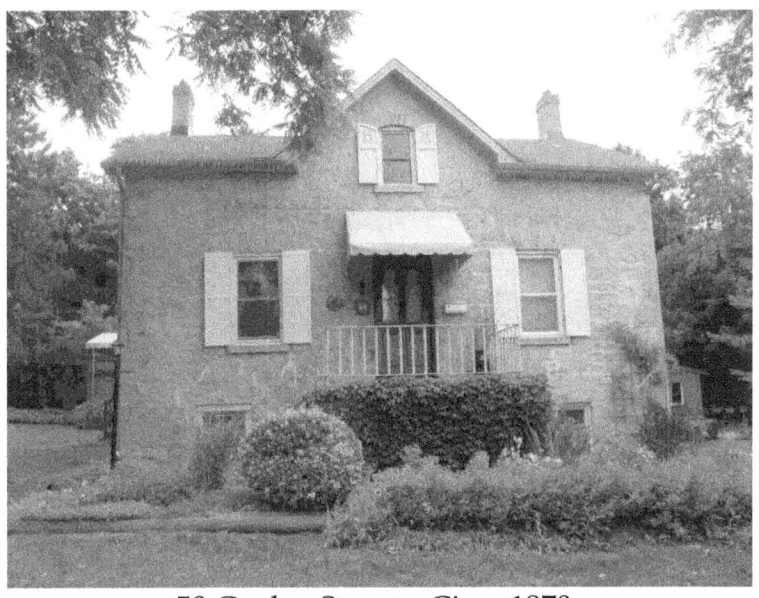

59 Cayley Street – Circa 1870s

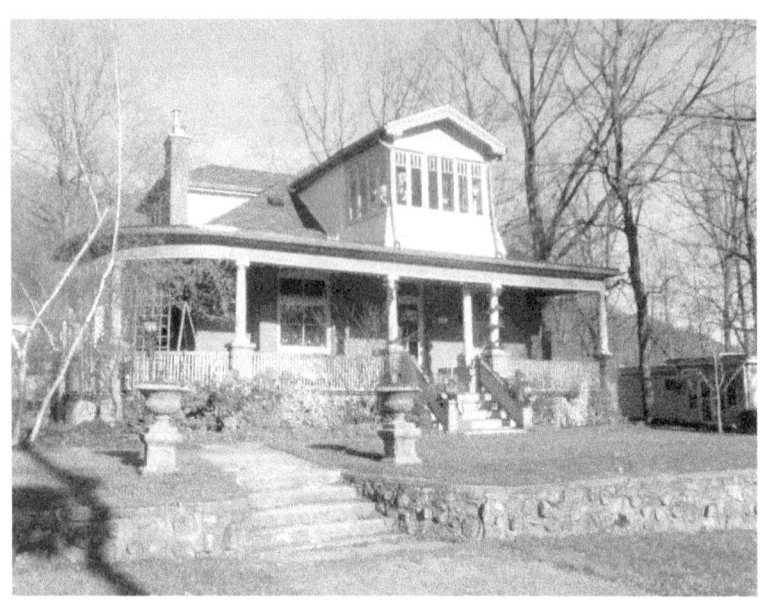

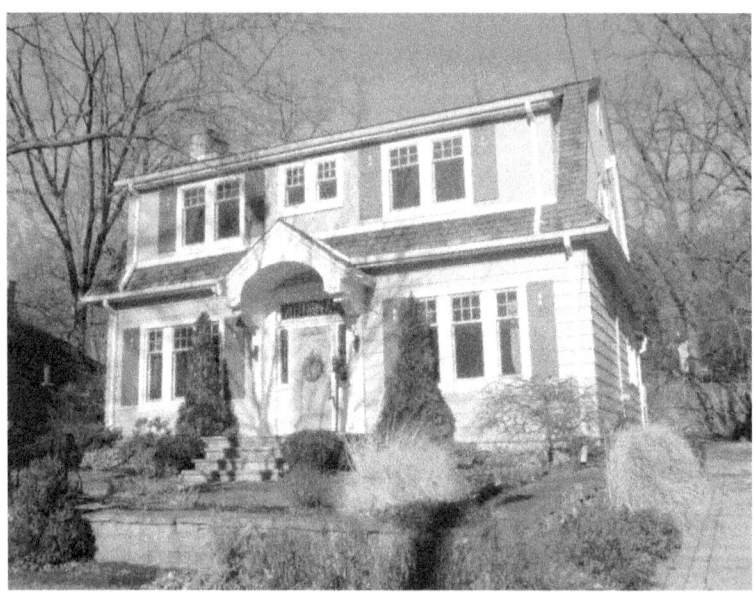

51 Cayley Street

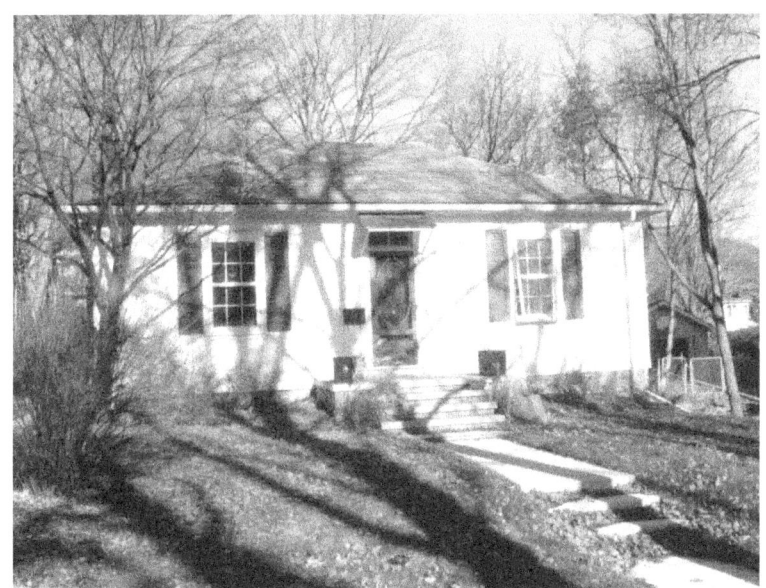

49 Cayley Street

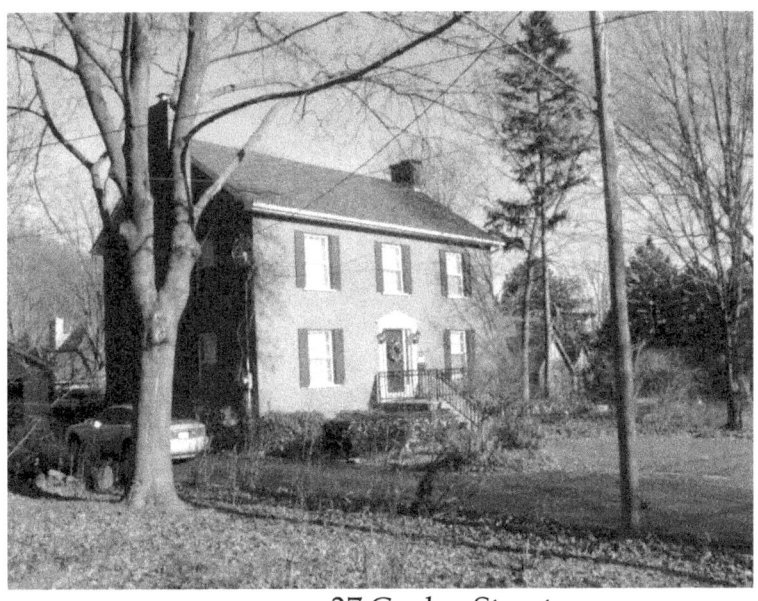

37 Cayley Street

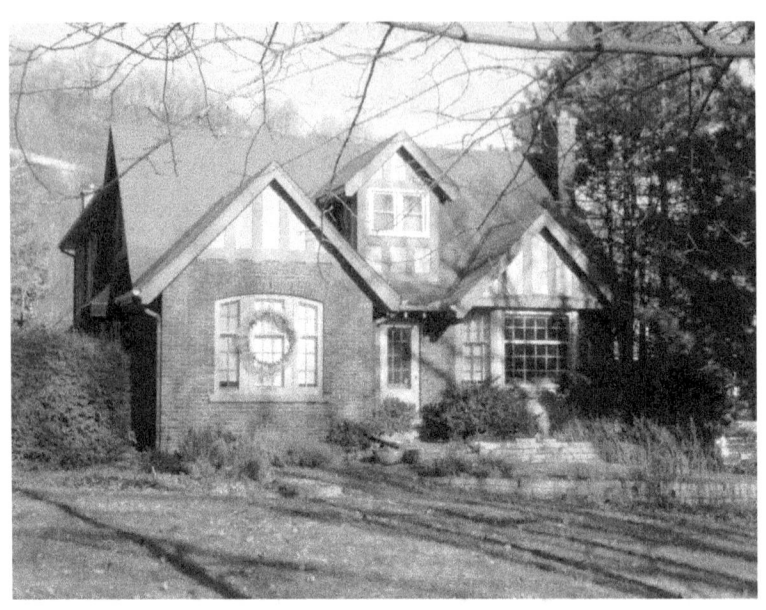

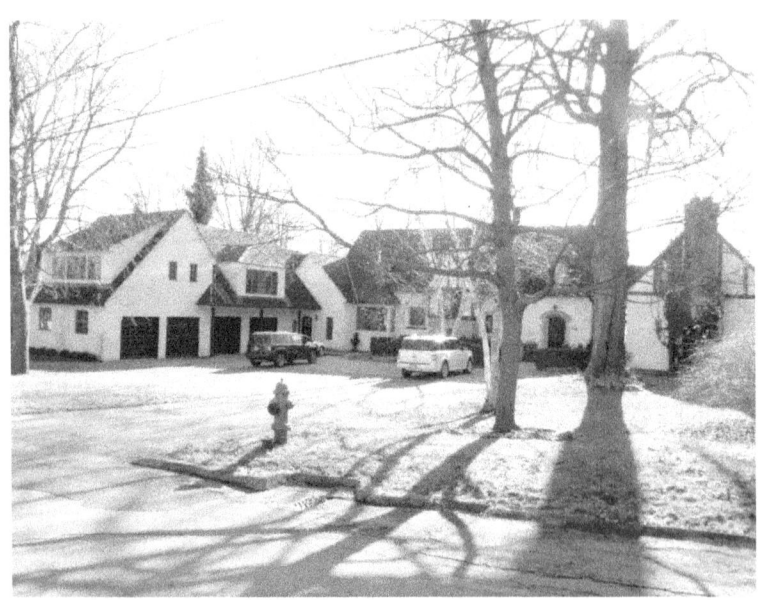

36 Cayley Street

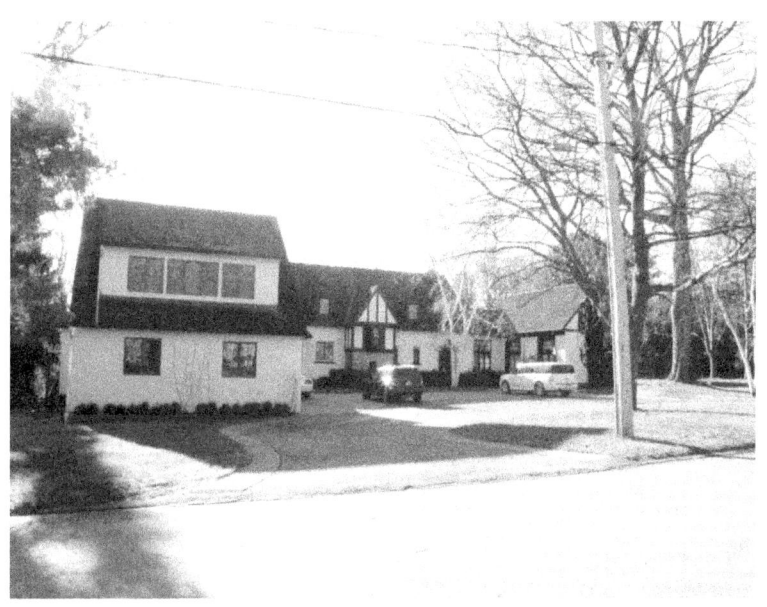

36 Cayley Street – three views

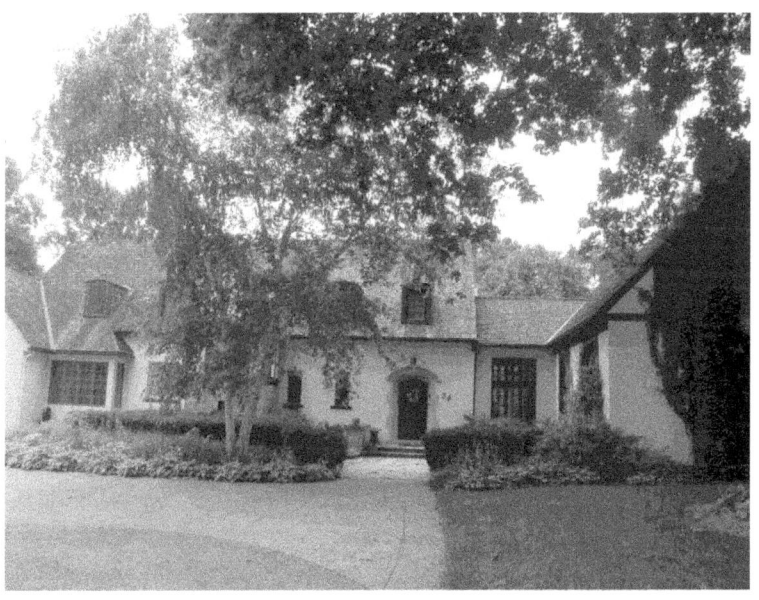

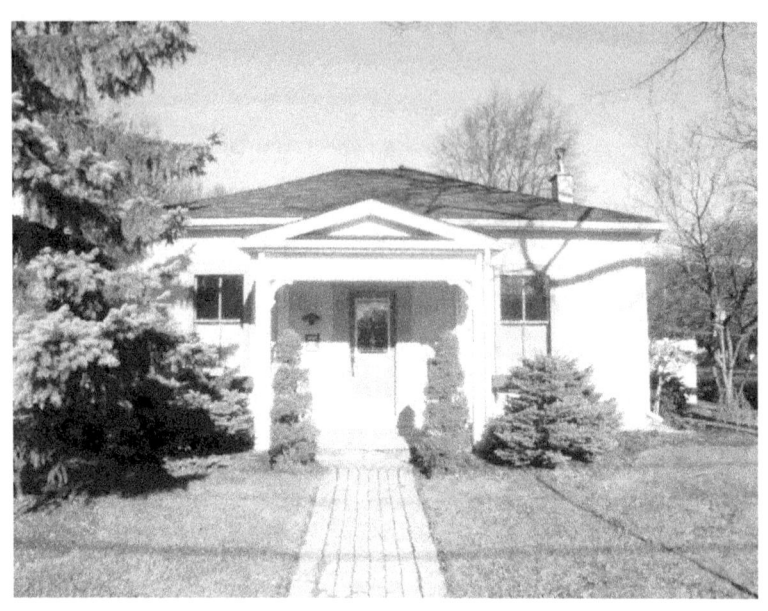

Parkview Street

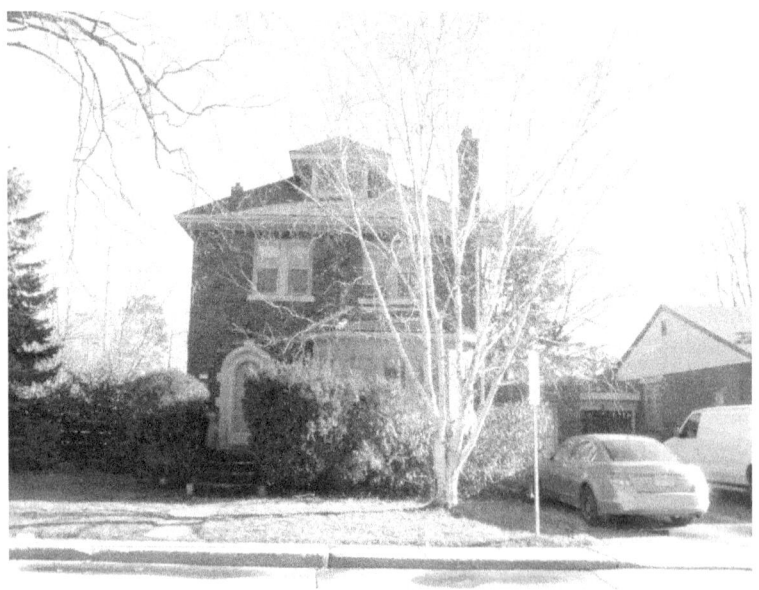

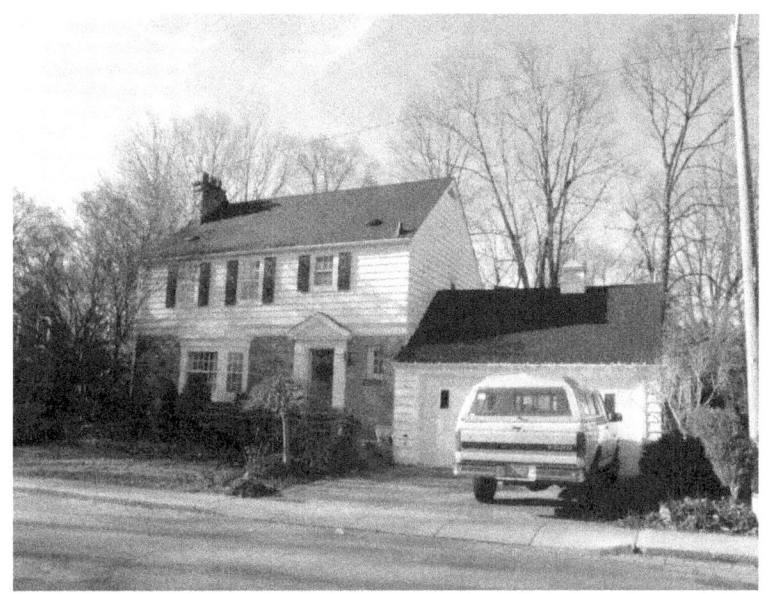

12 Parkview Street

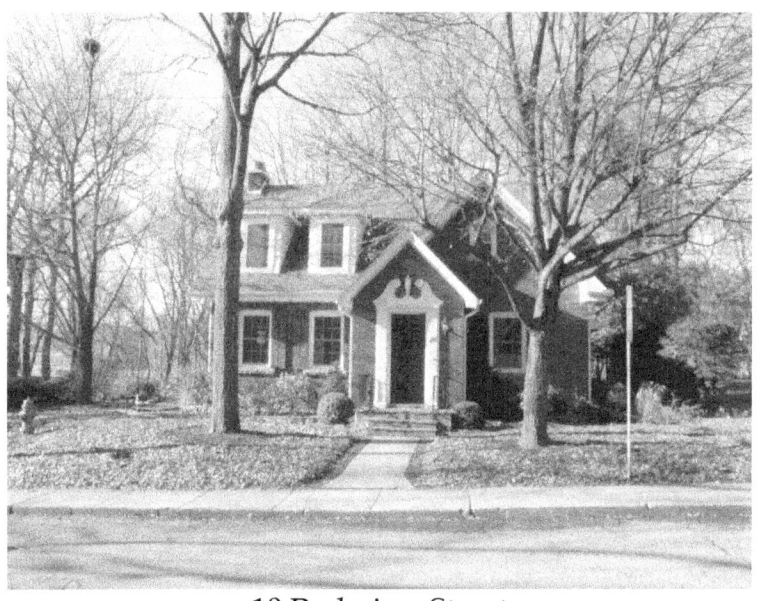

10 Parkview Street

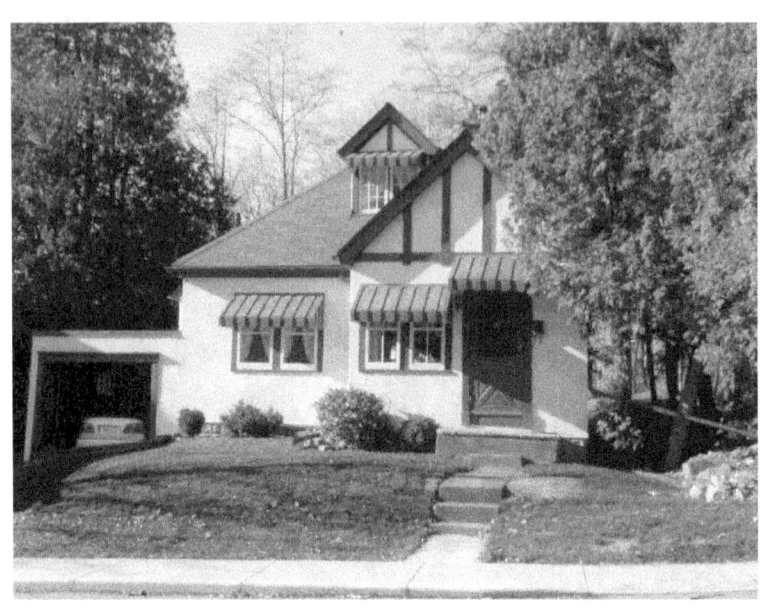

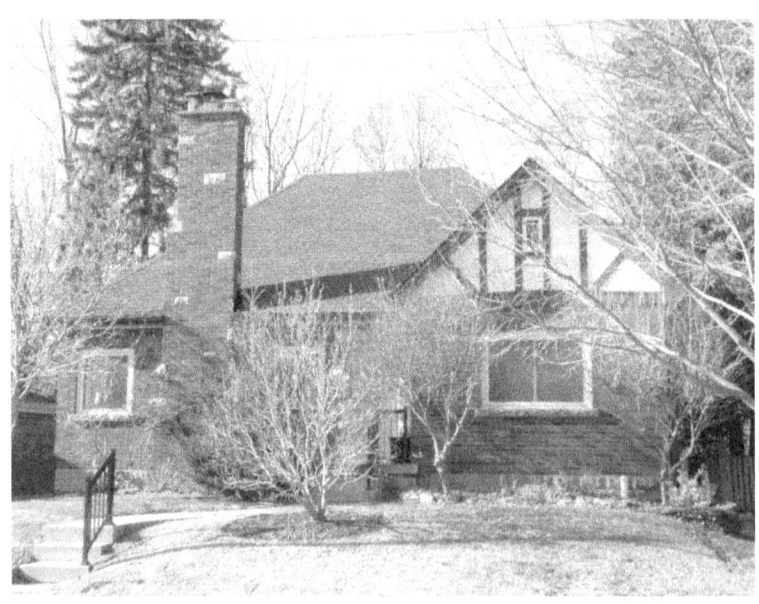

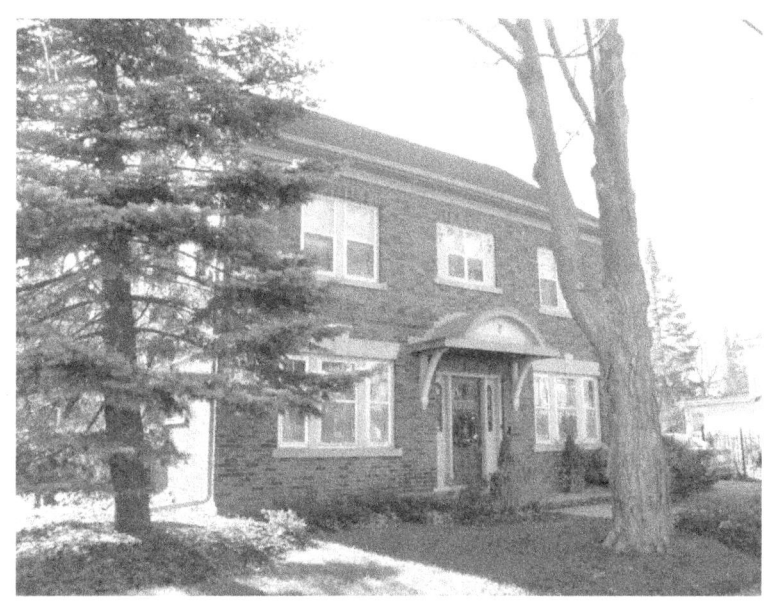

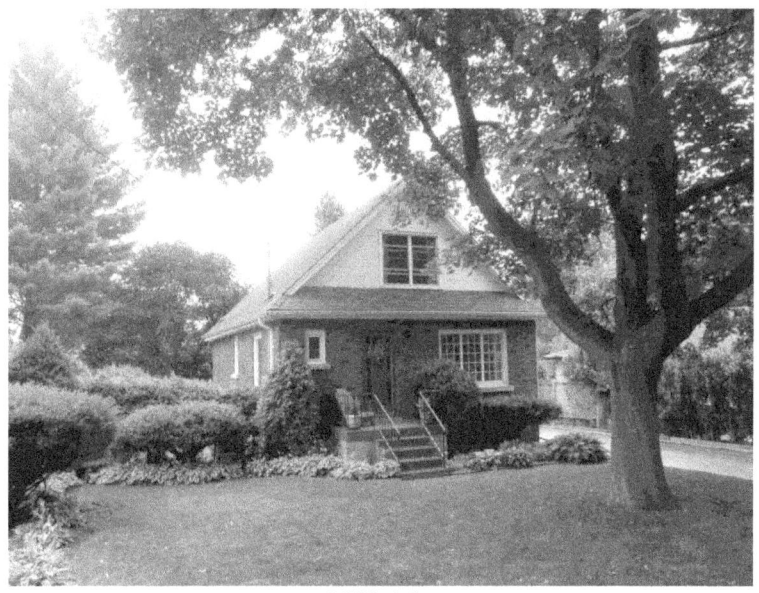

Hillside

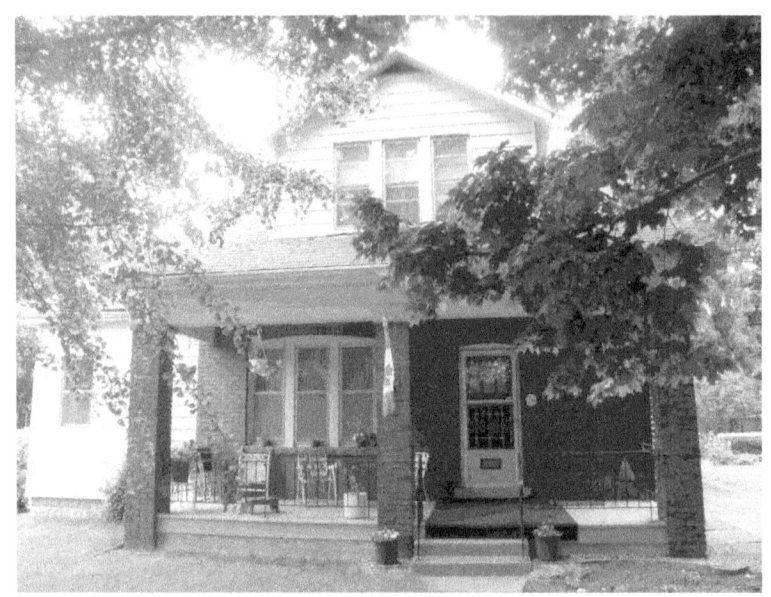

30 Hillside – built early 1930s

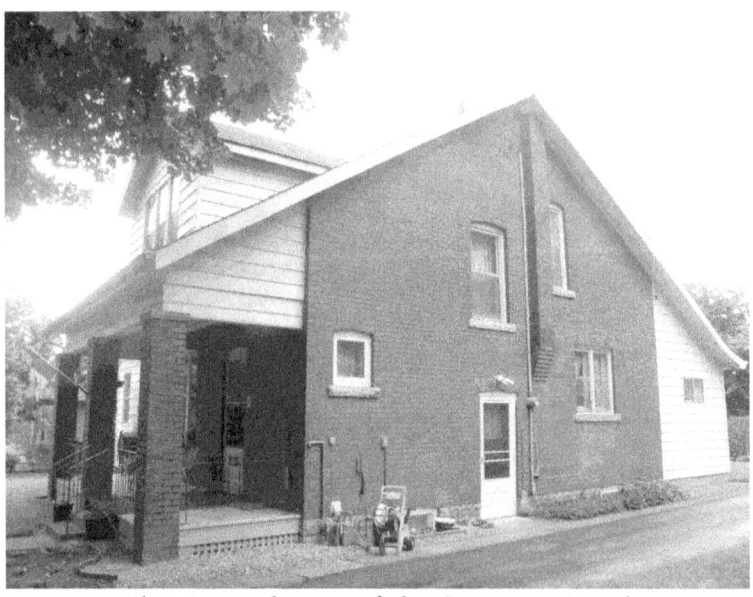

side view – home of the Stewart Family

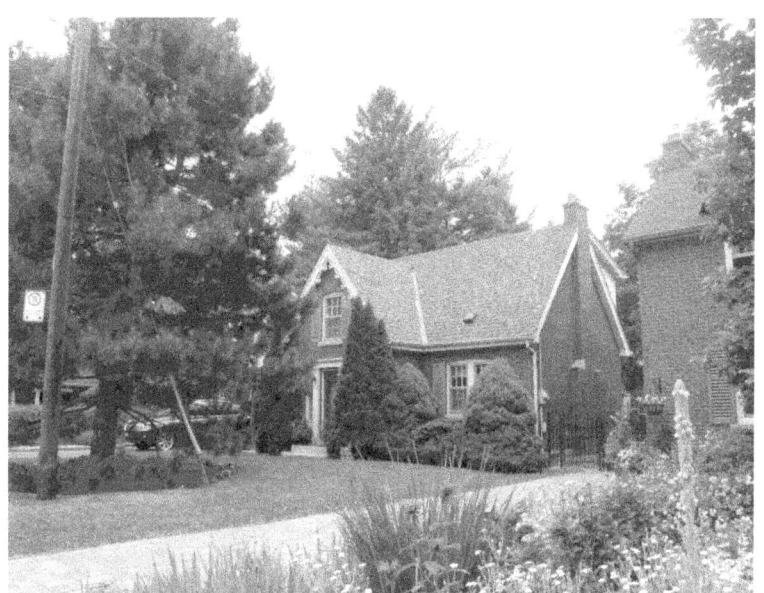

Gingerbread trim on the gable

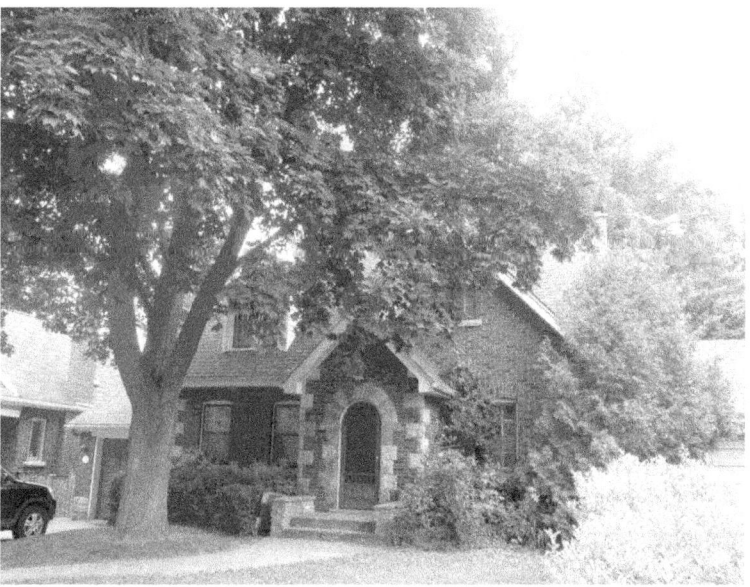

Different coloured brick gives a decorative finish
around the entrance

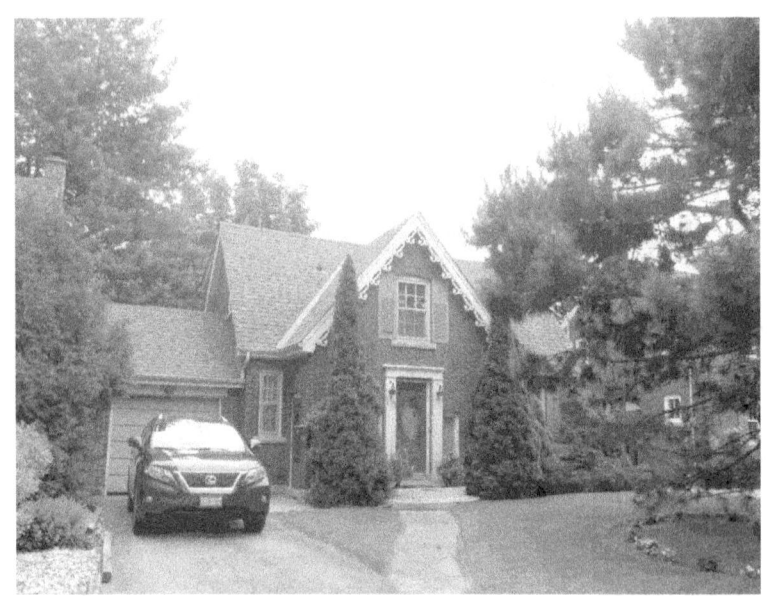

13 Hillside

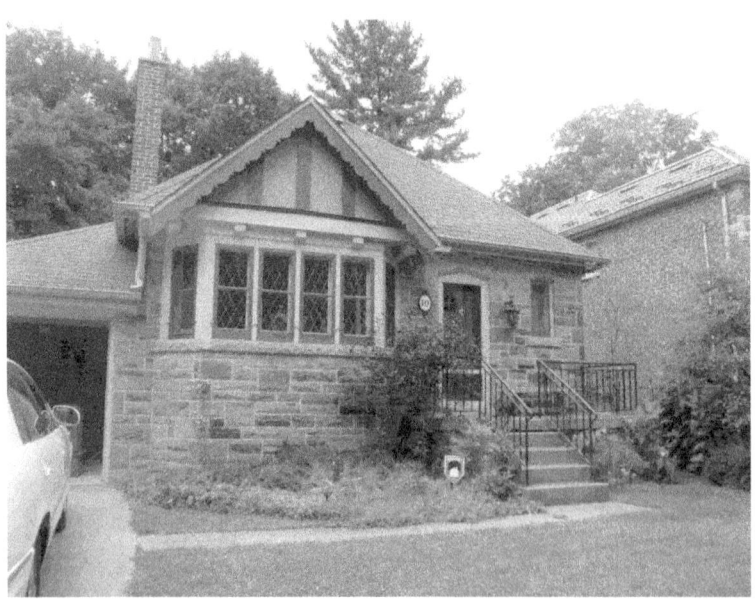

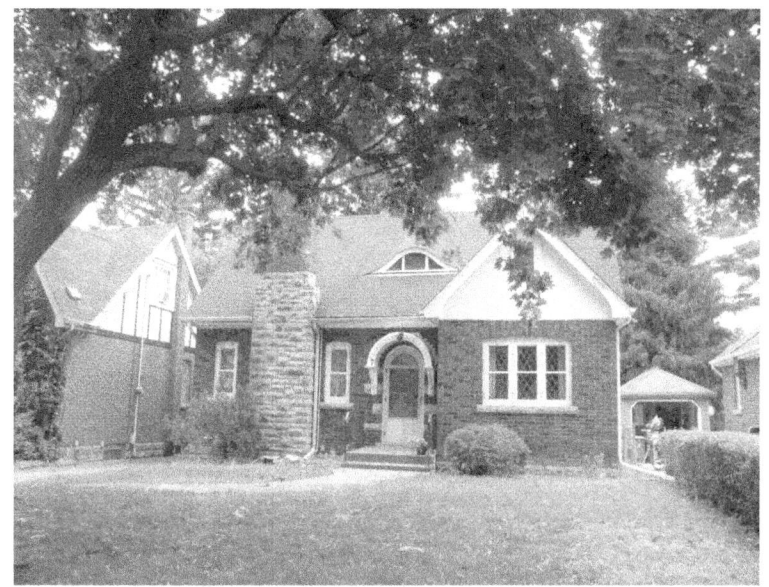

7 Hillside

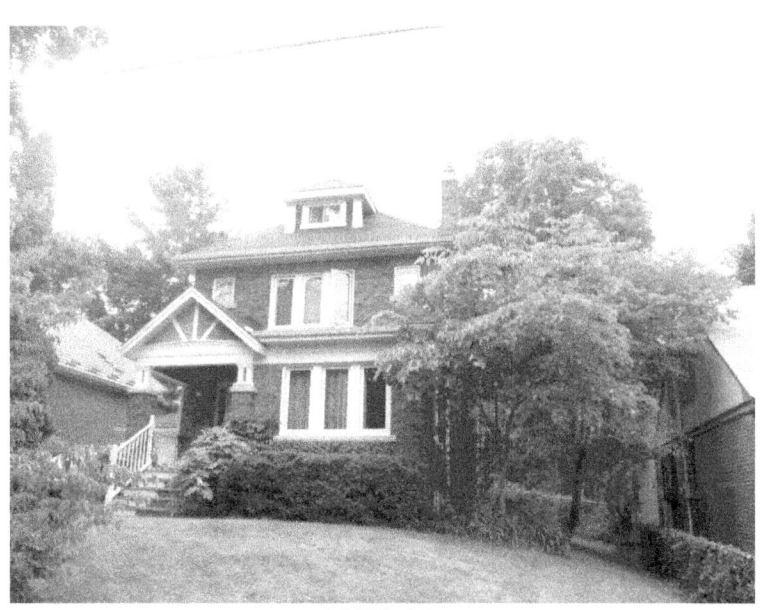

6 Hillside

South Street Area

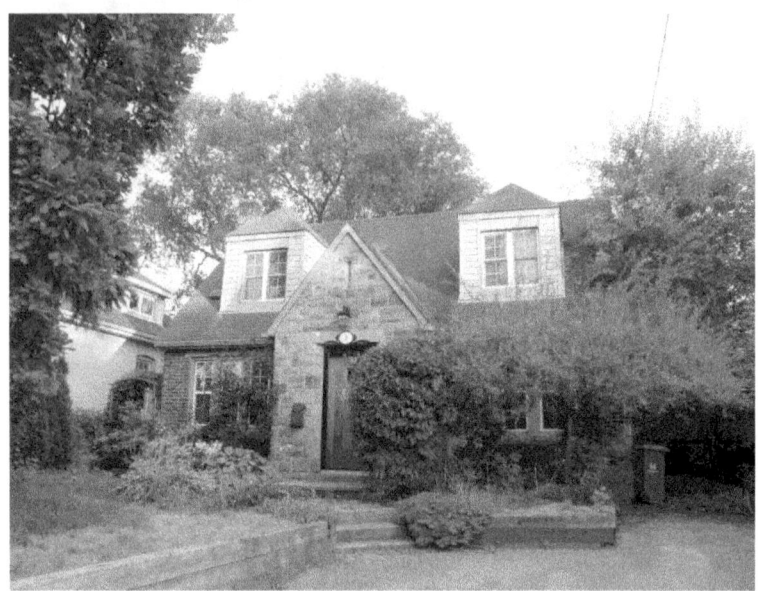

3 South Street

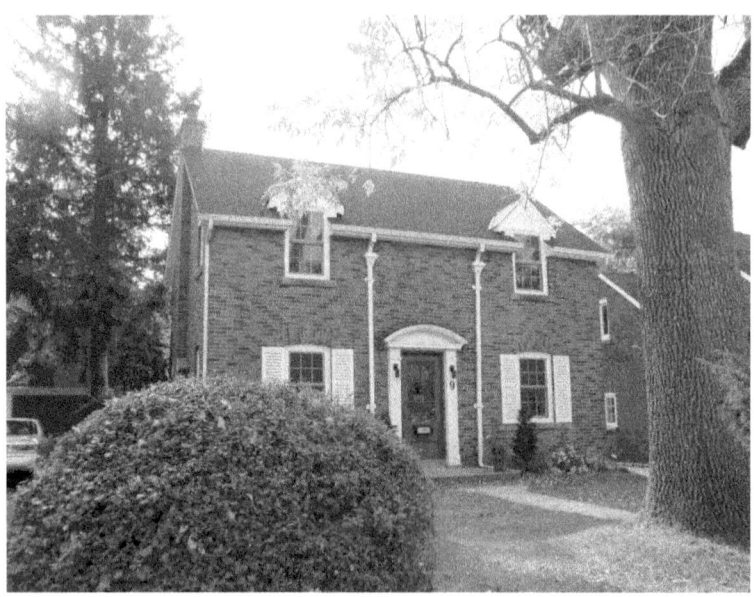

9 South Street

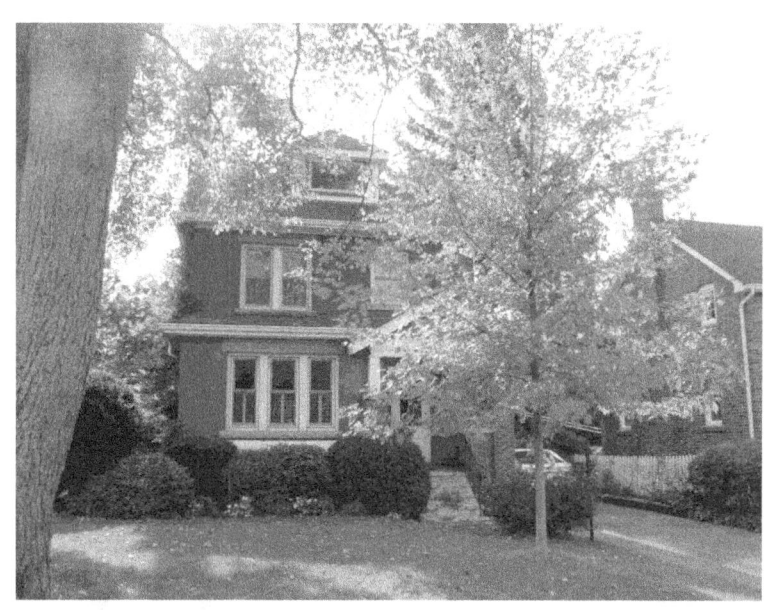

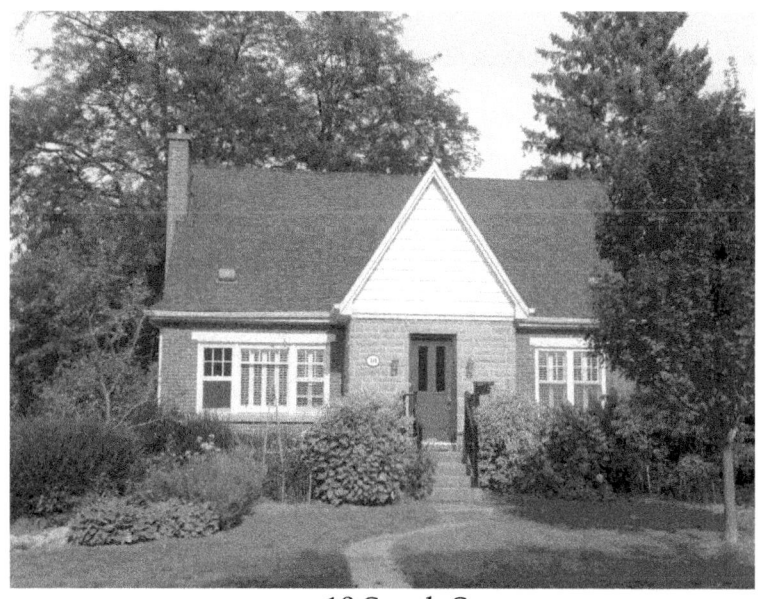

10 South Street

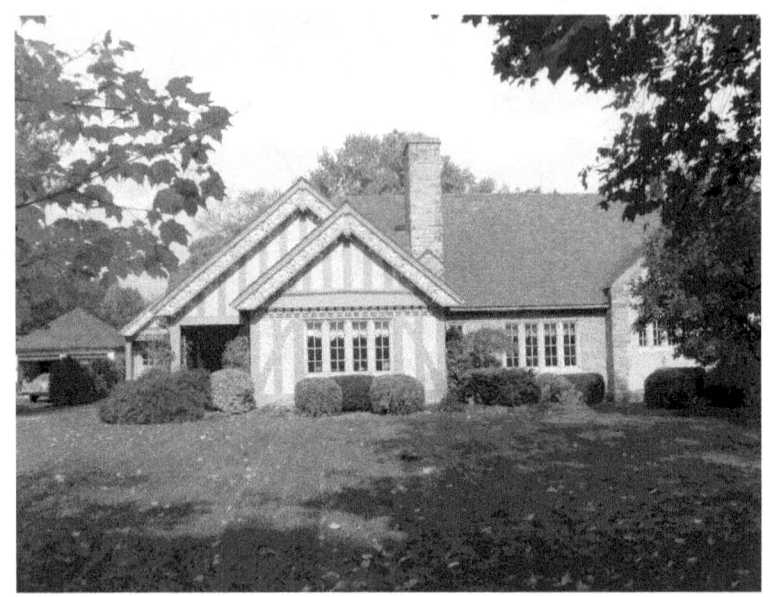

67 South Street

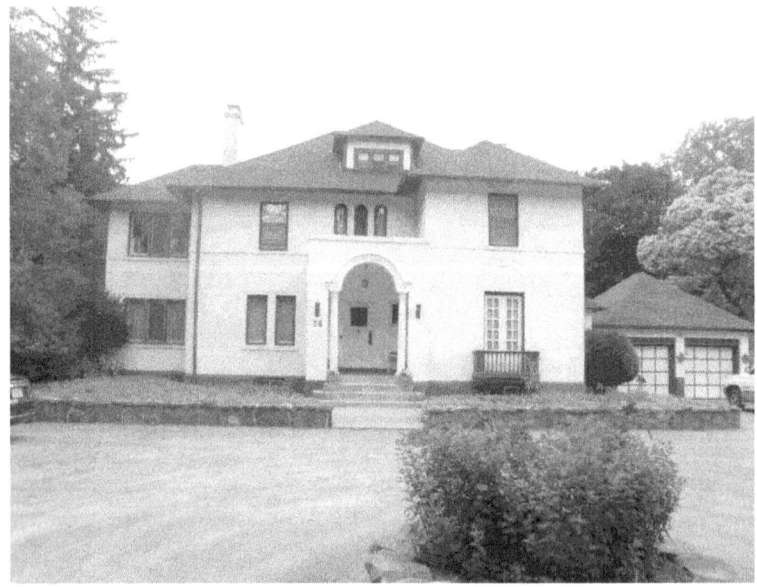

24 South Street

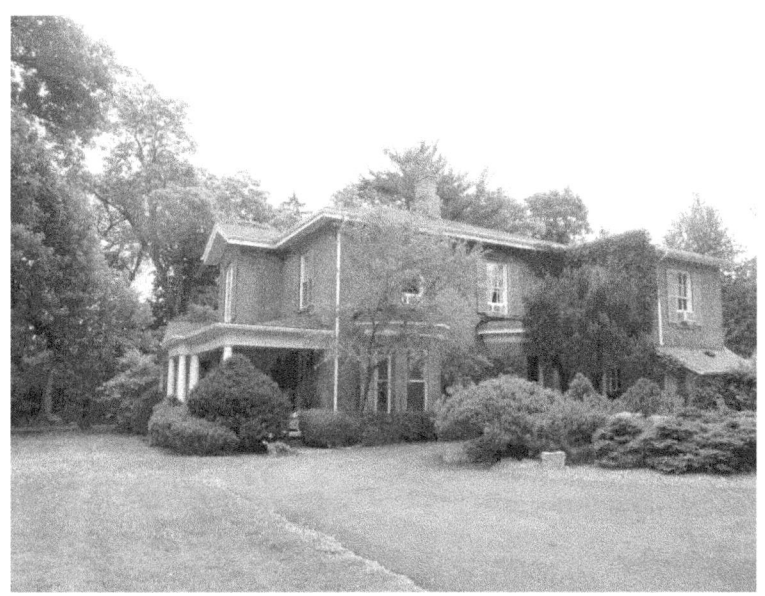

30 South Street – Osler House – circa 1848

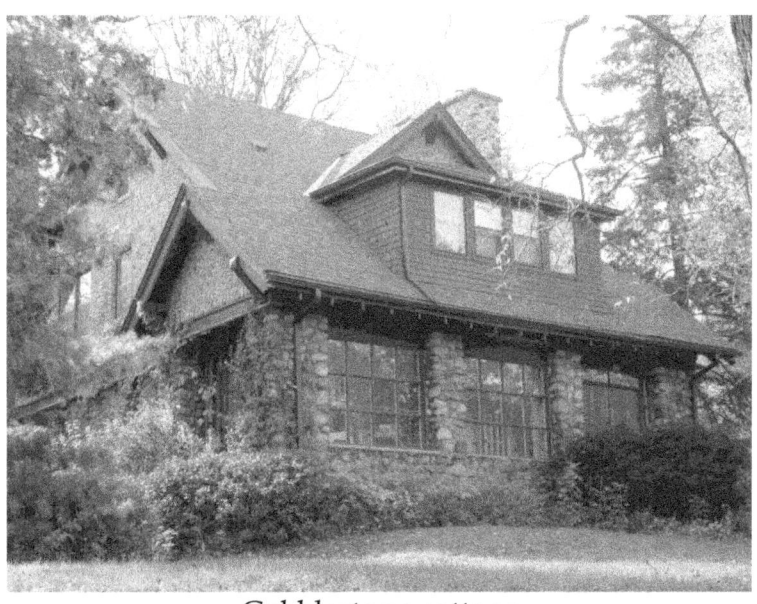

Cobblestone cottage

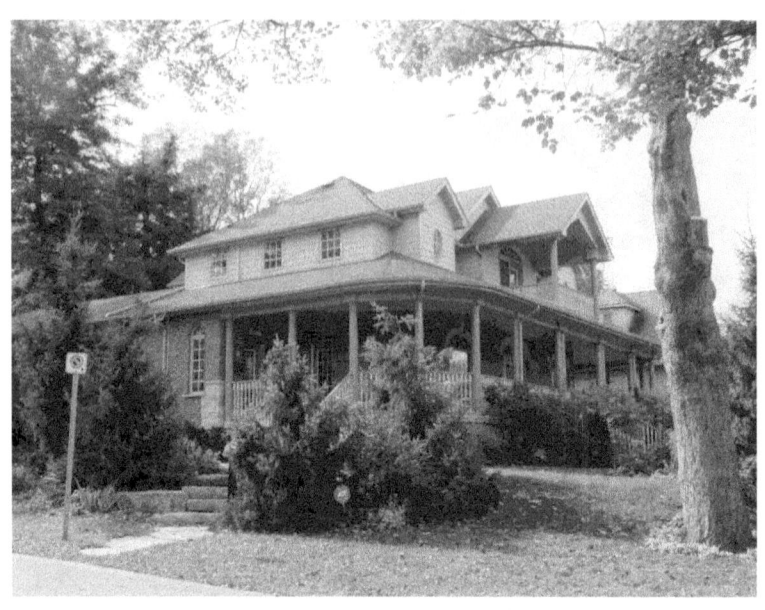

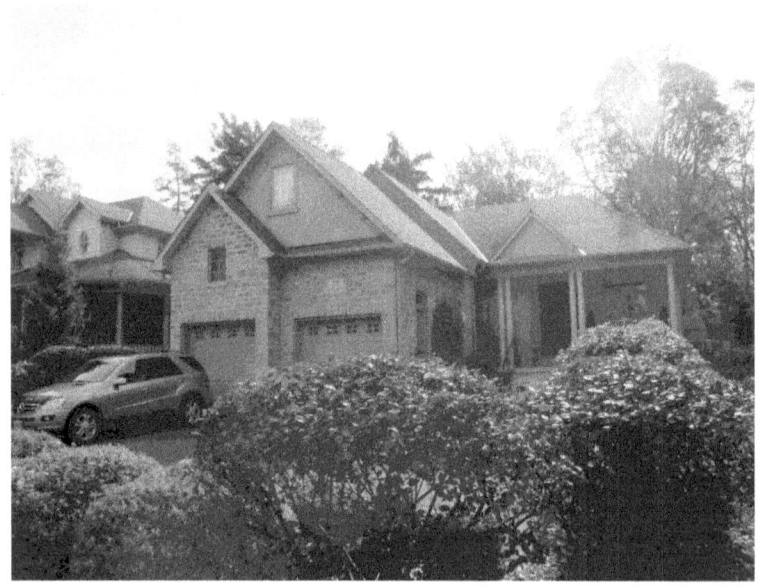

31 South Street

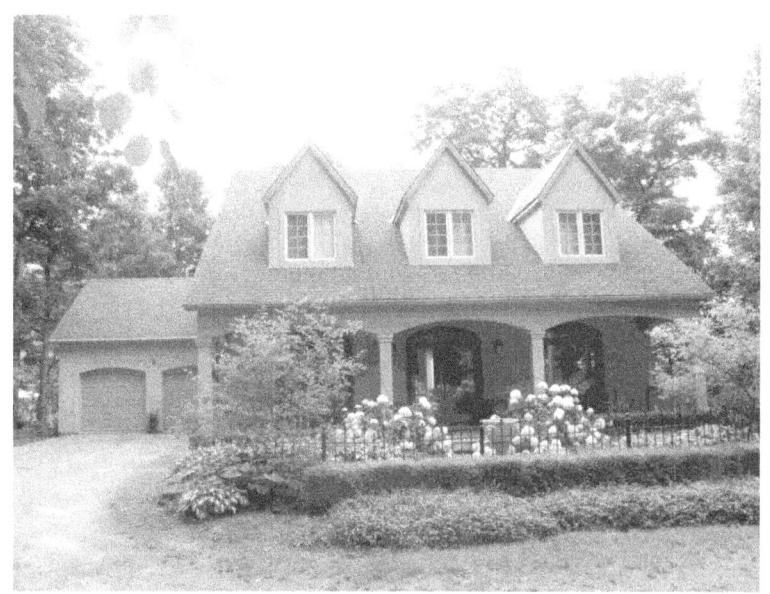

9 Hatfield

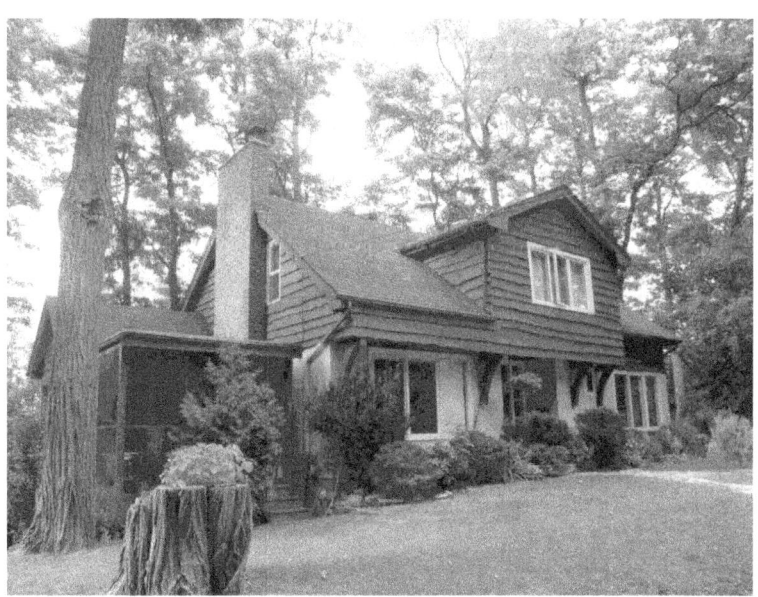

7 Hatfield

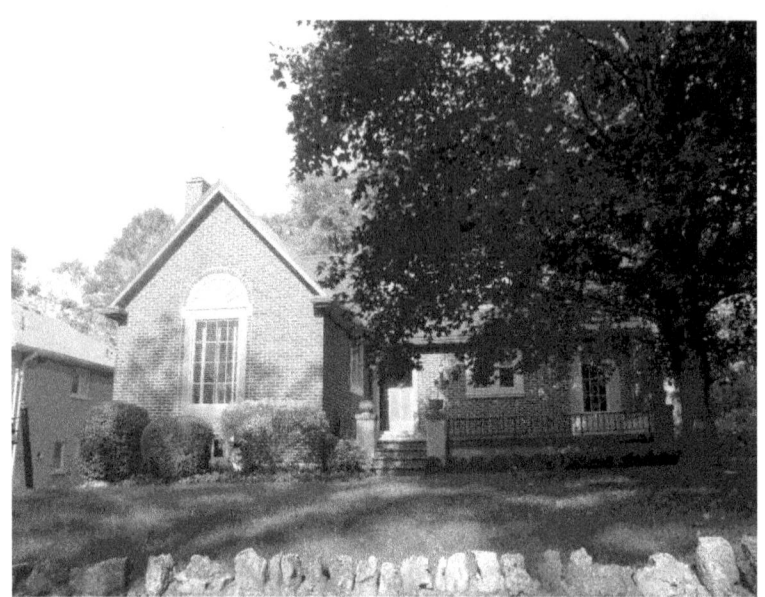

64 South Street - Devon Cottage

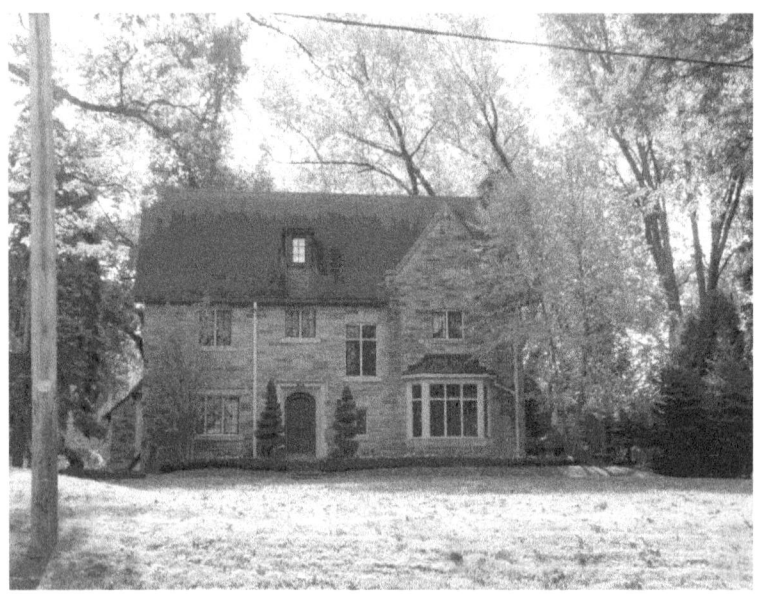

53 South Street

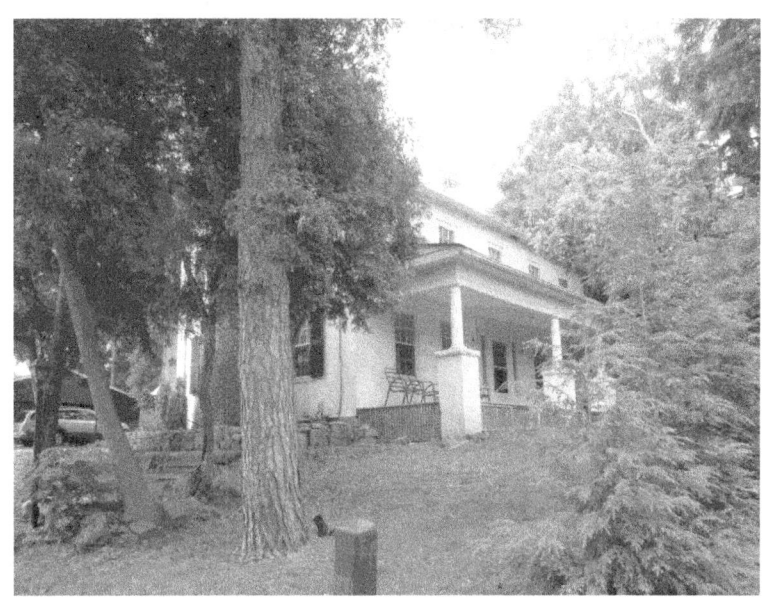

6 Woodward

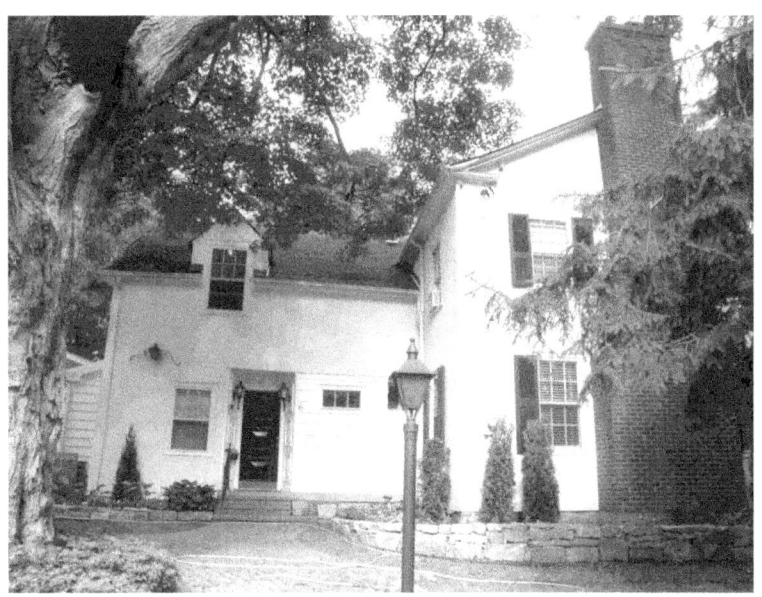

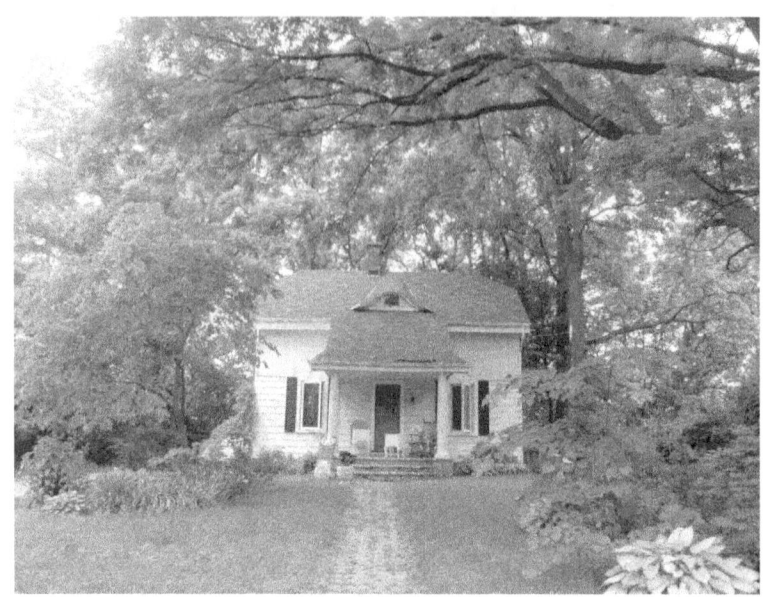

10 Woodward

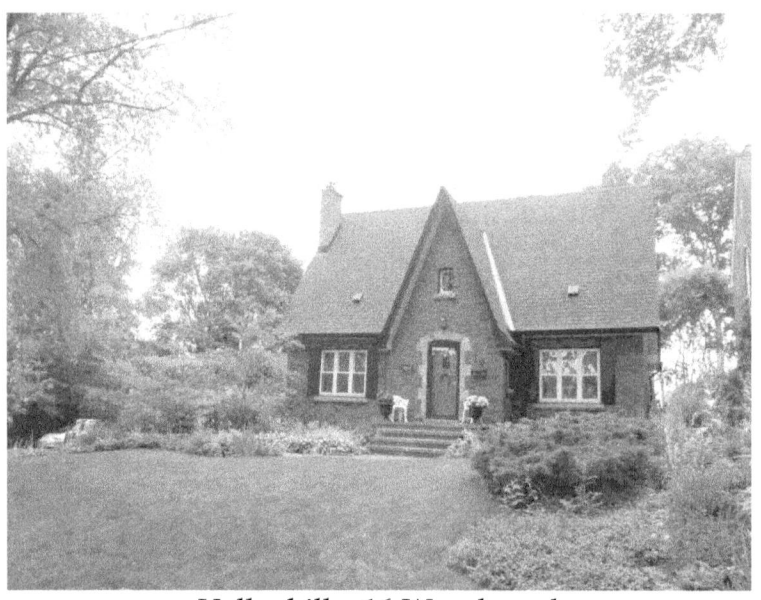

Valleyhill – 16 Woodward

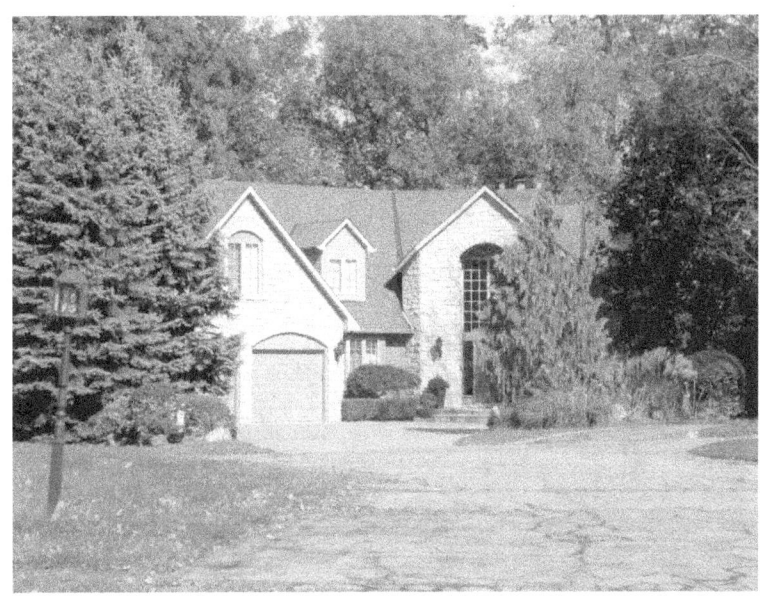

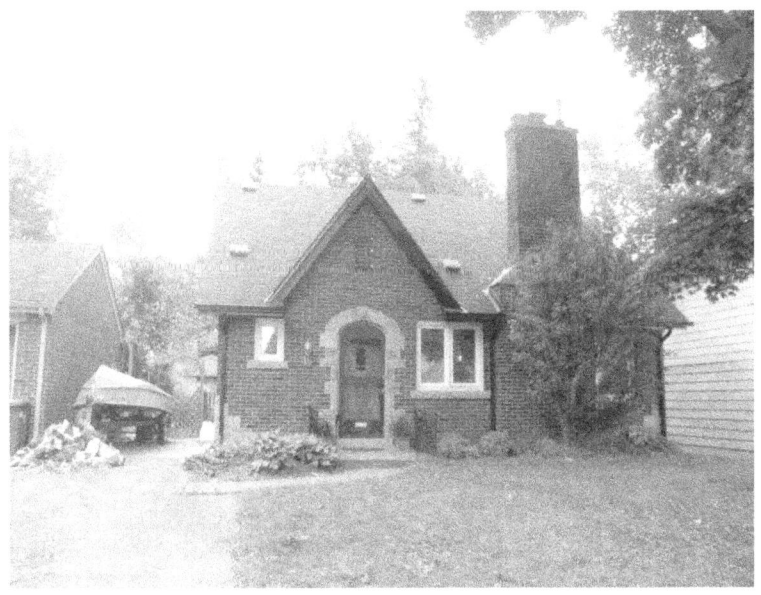

#16

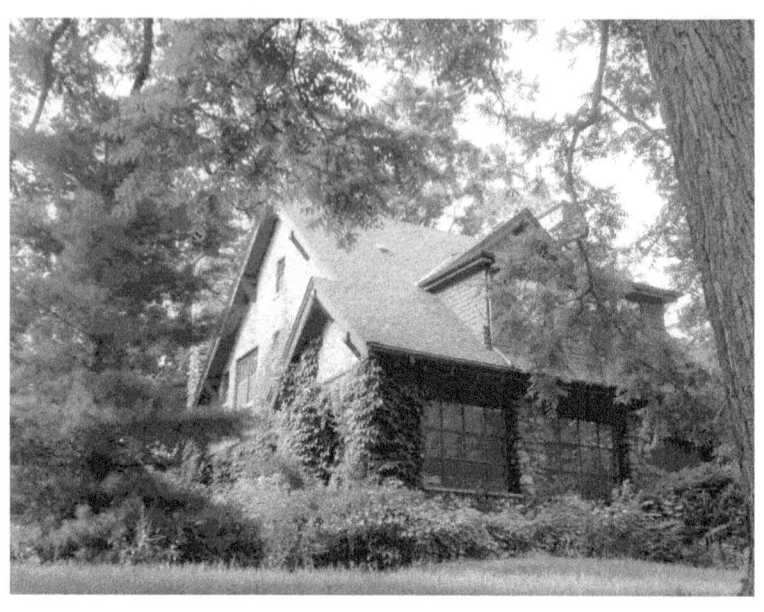

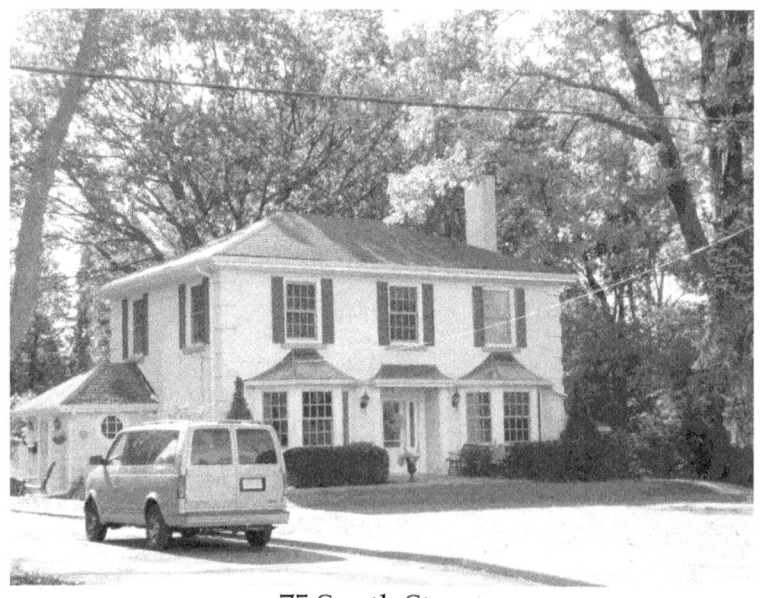

75 South Street

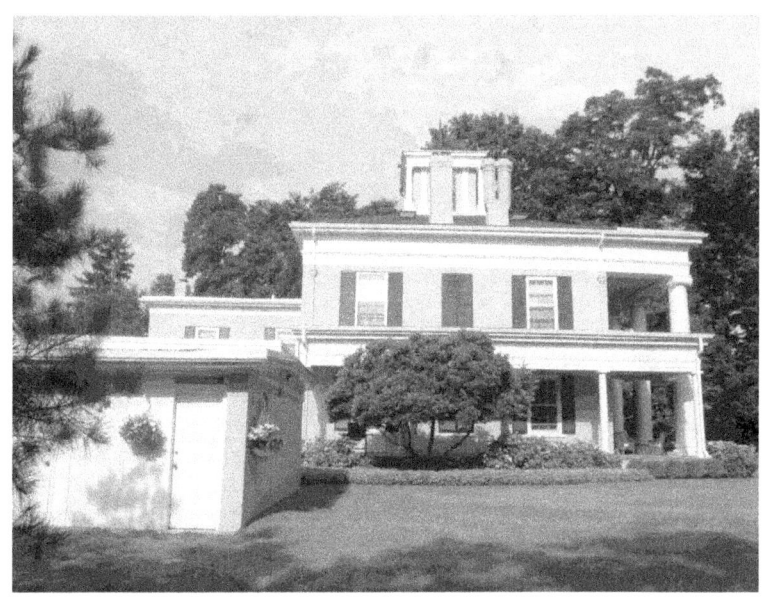

South Street

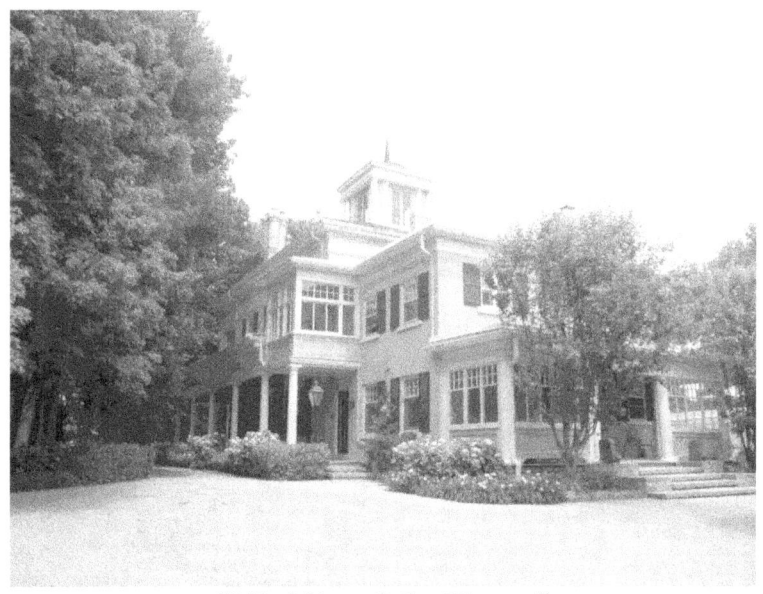

"Wedding Cake House"

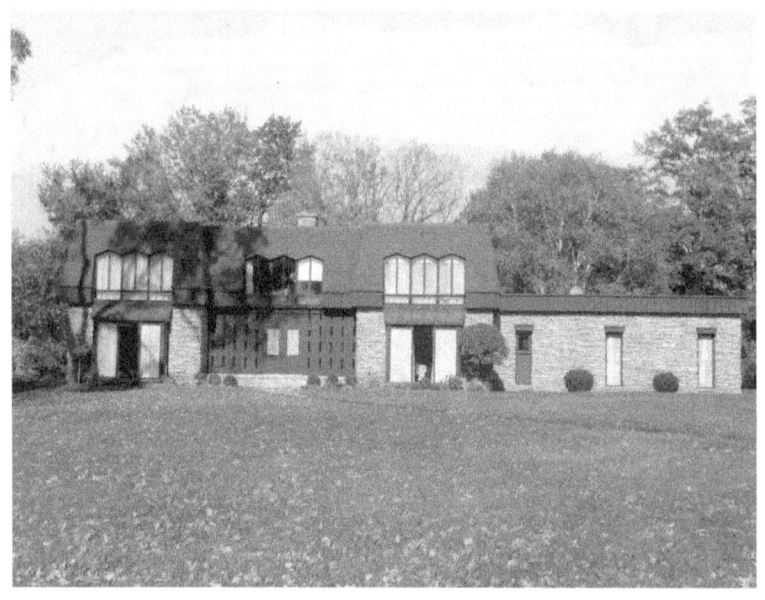

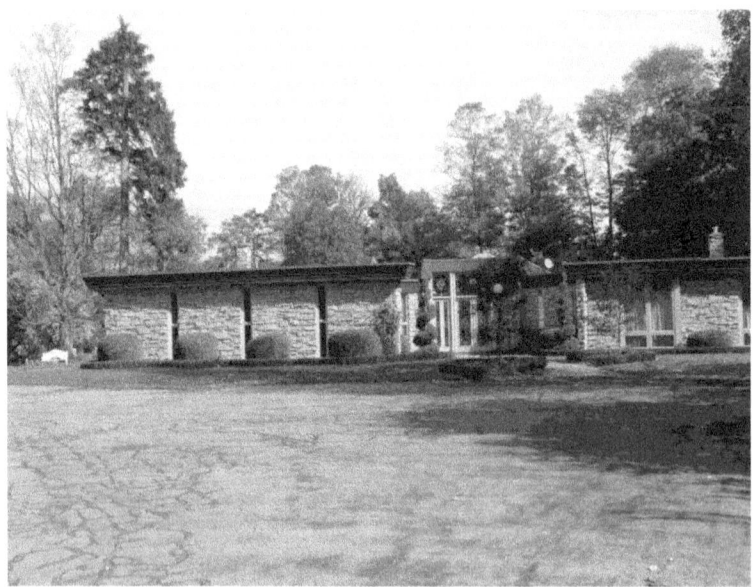

66 South Street

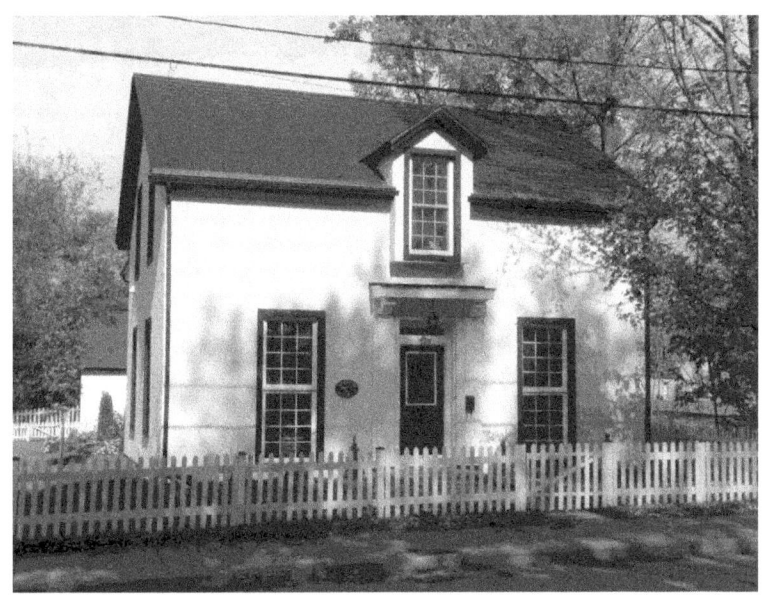

Southend - 72 South Street

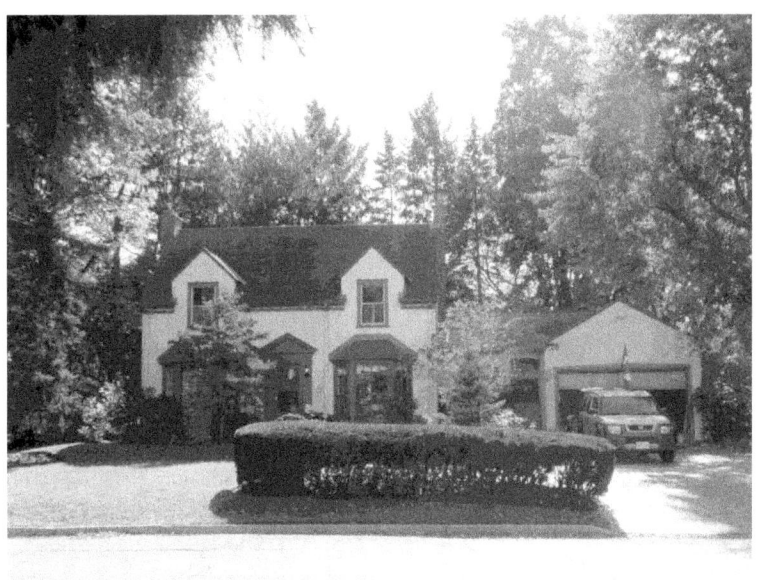

Two Gothic style gables

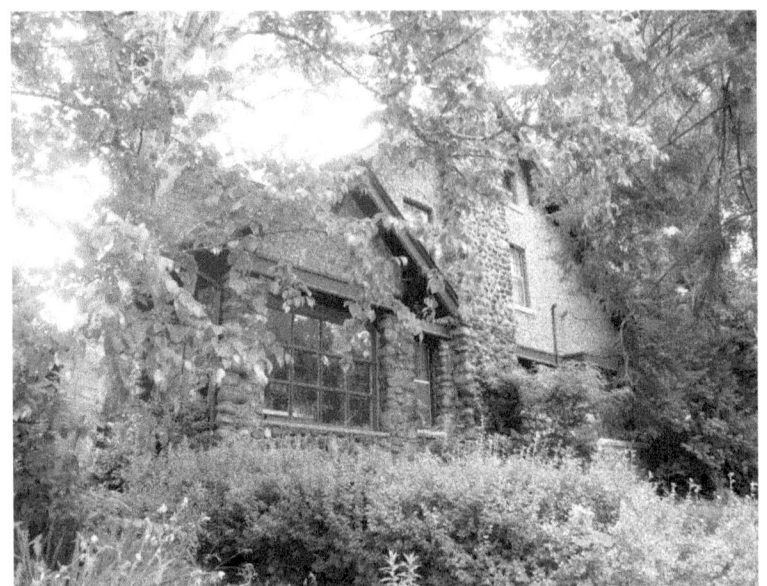

Cobblestone cottage

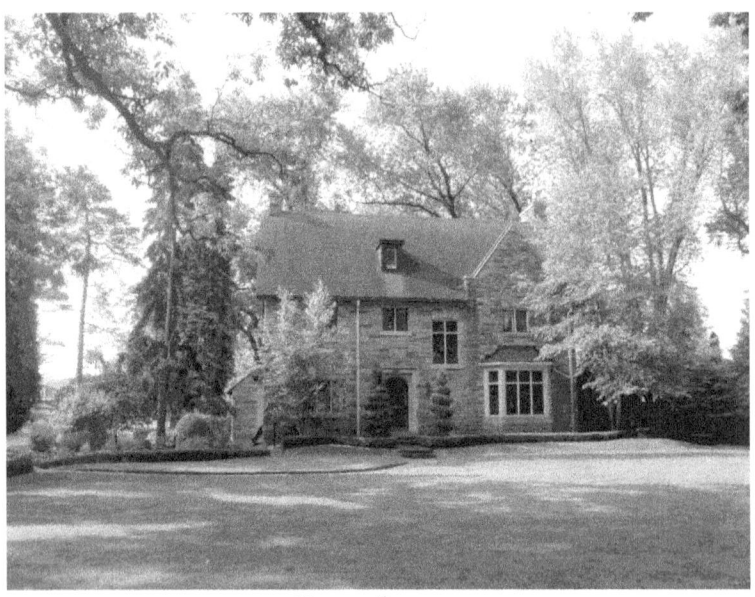

Stone house

Old Ancaster Road was the main road between
Dundas and Ancaster in the early 1800s

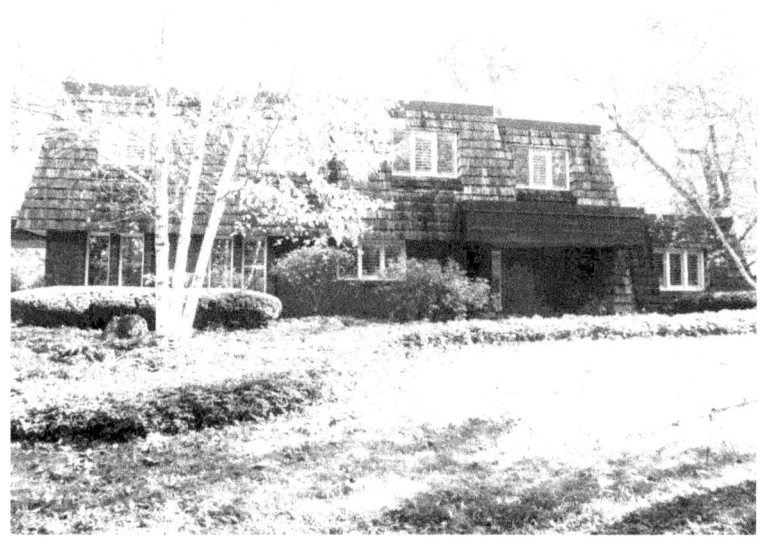

14 Old Ancaster Road

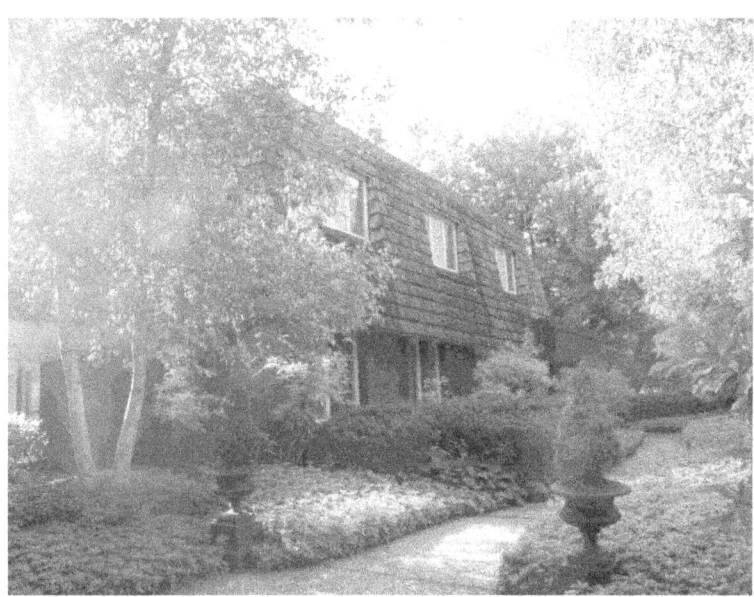

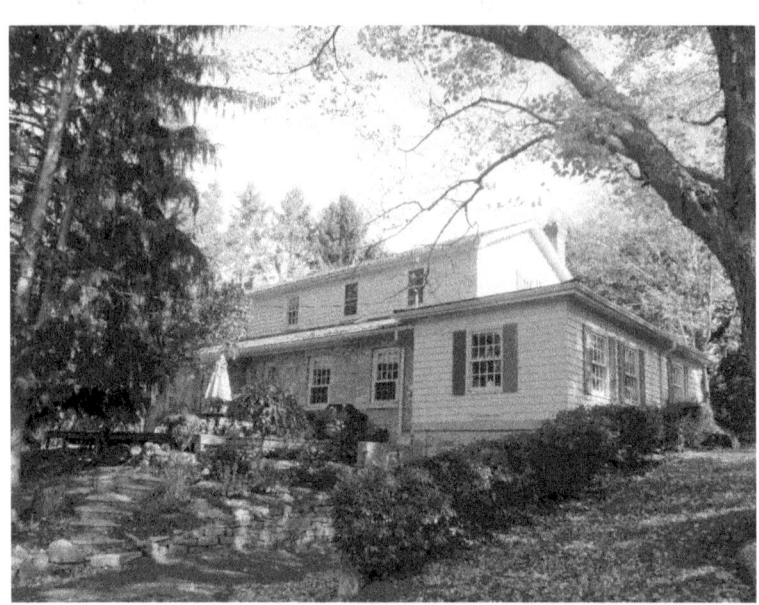

Back – 2nd storey added in 1950
12 Old Ancaster Road

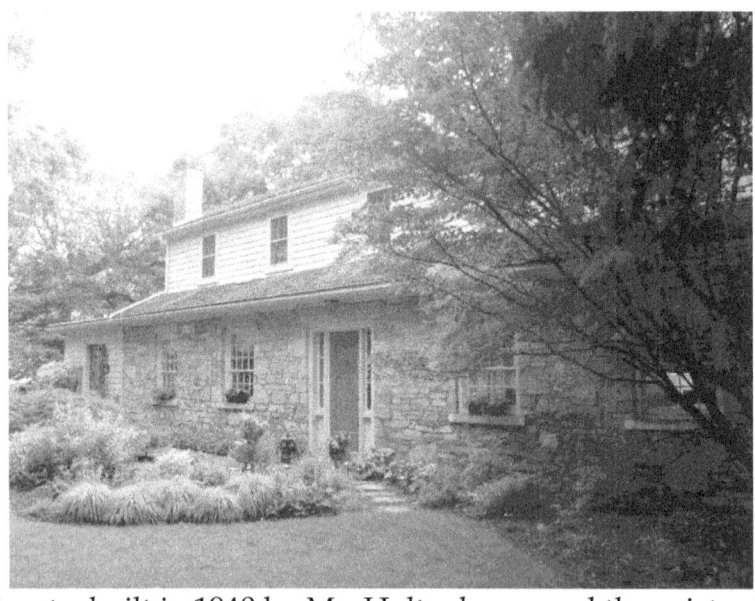

Front – built in 1940 by Mr. Holt who owned the grist mill
and brewery down the hill in Dundas

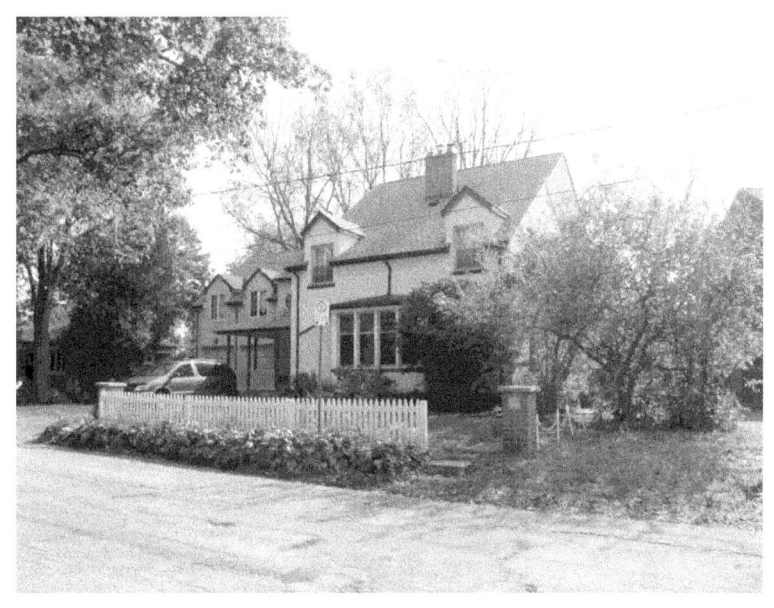

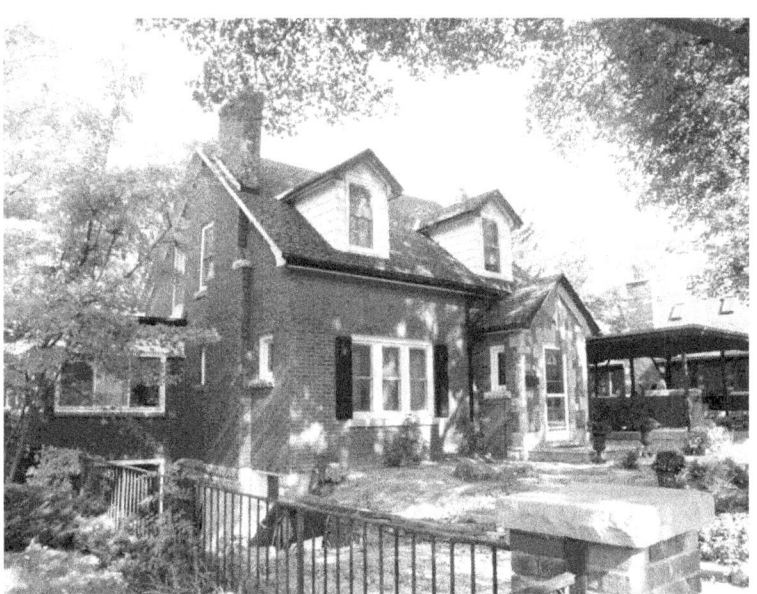

#4

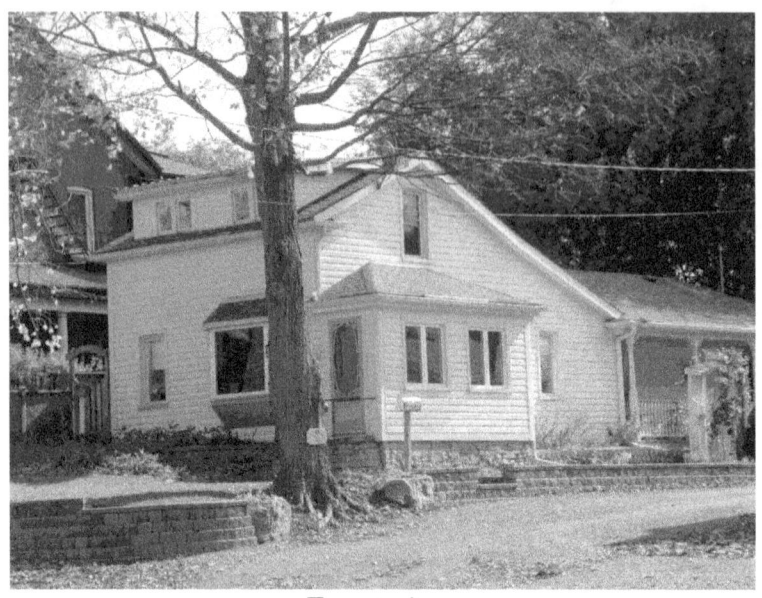

Front view

#45 – two views

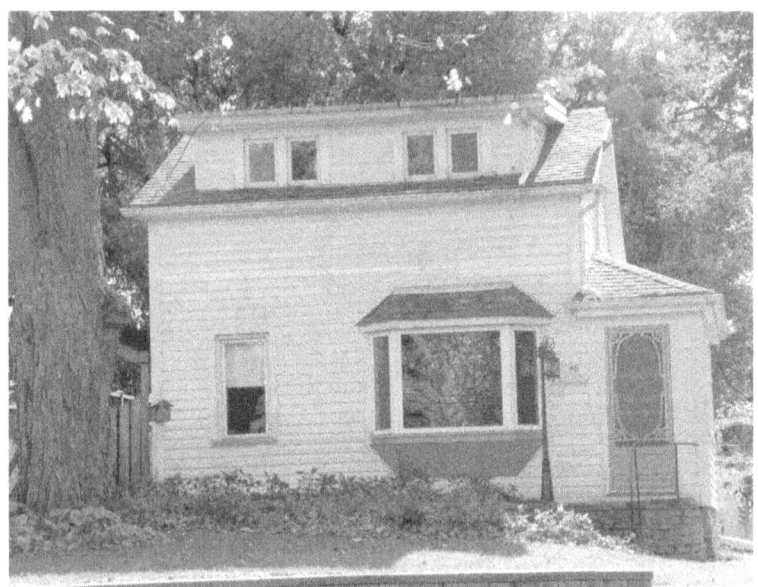

End view

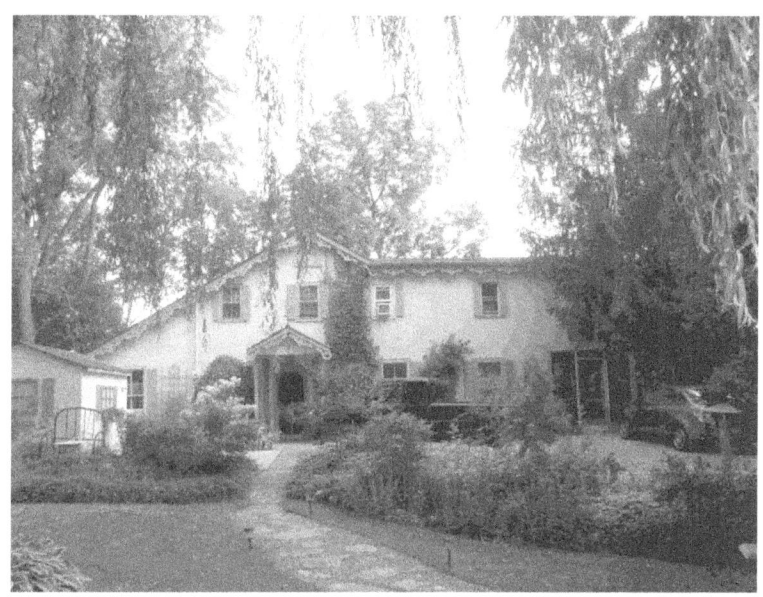

42 Osler Drive – a Bed and Breakfast called Glenwood

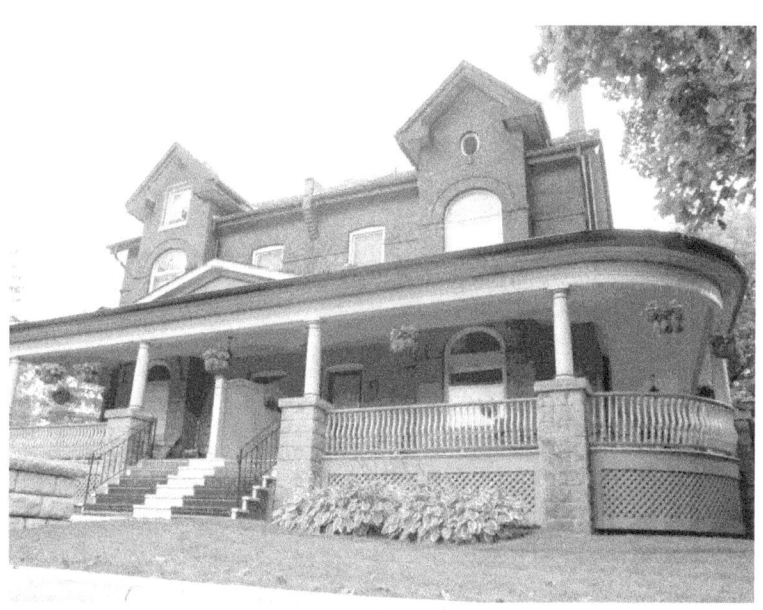

47 & 49 Osler

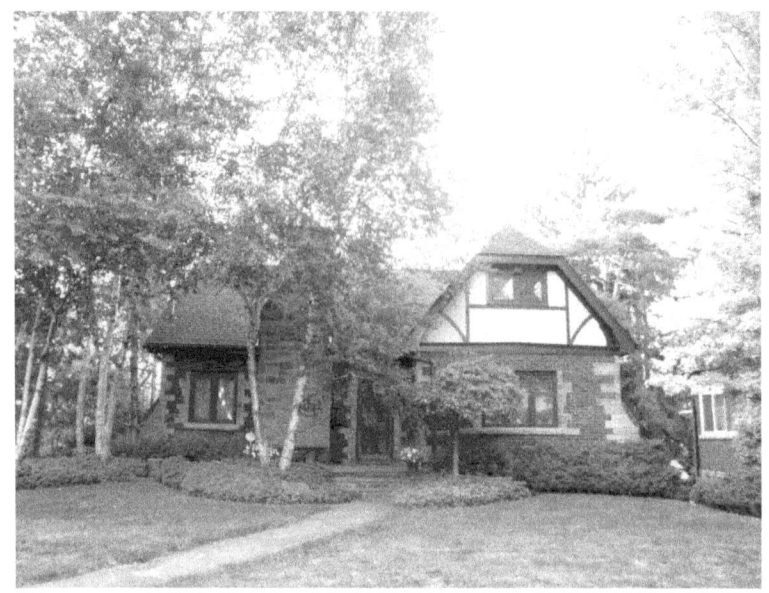

2 Ancaster Street

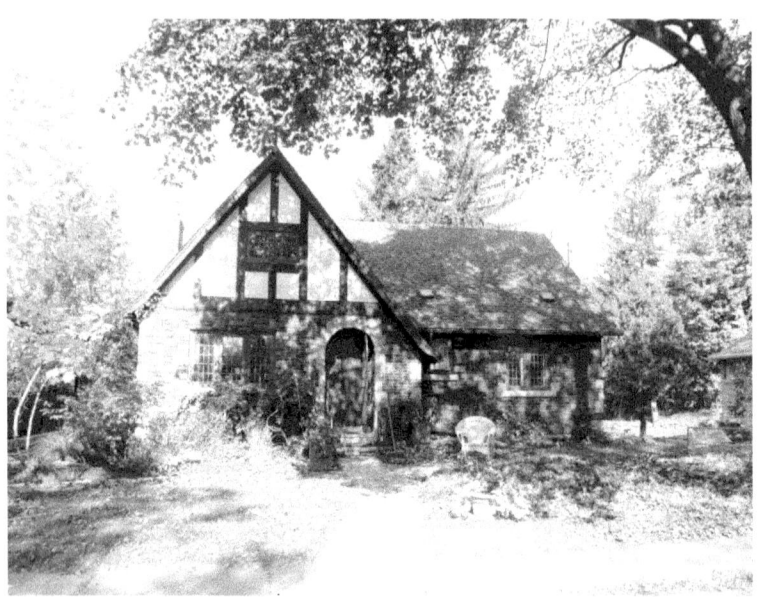

6 Ancaster Street

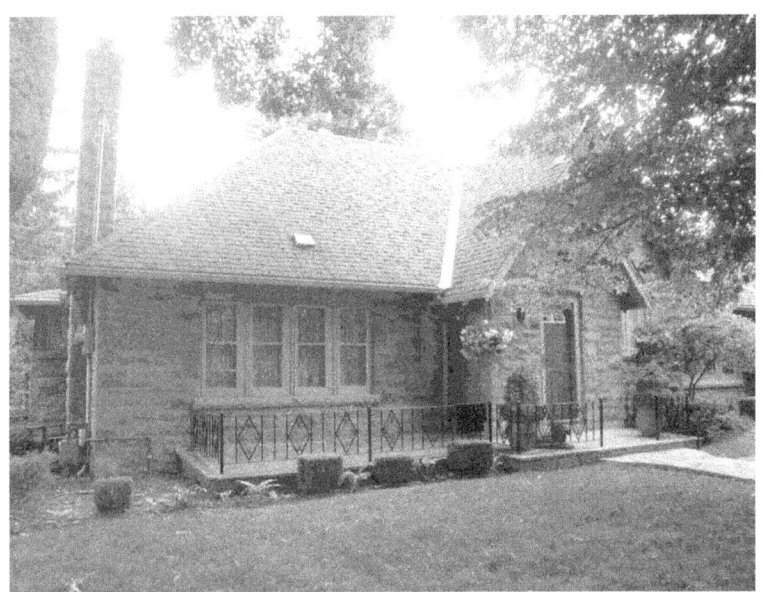

8 Ancaster Street

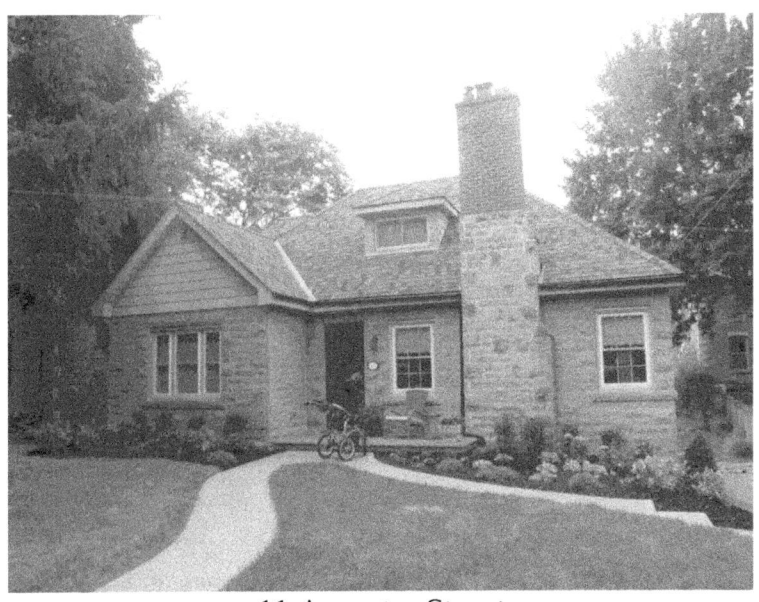

11 Ancaster Street

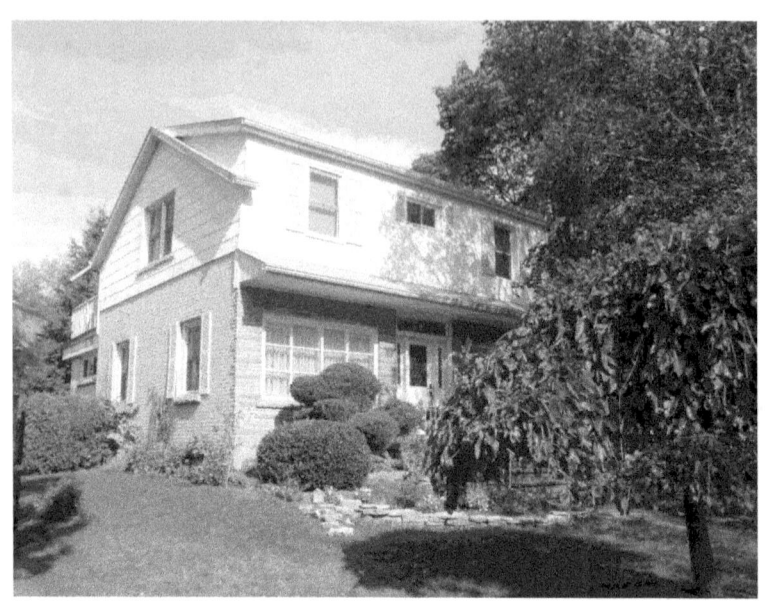

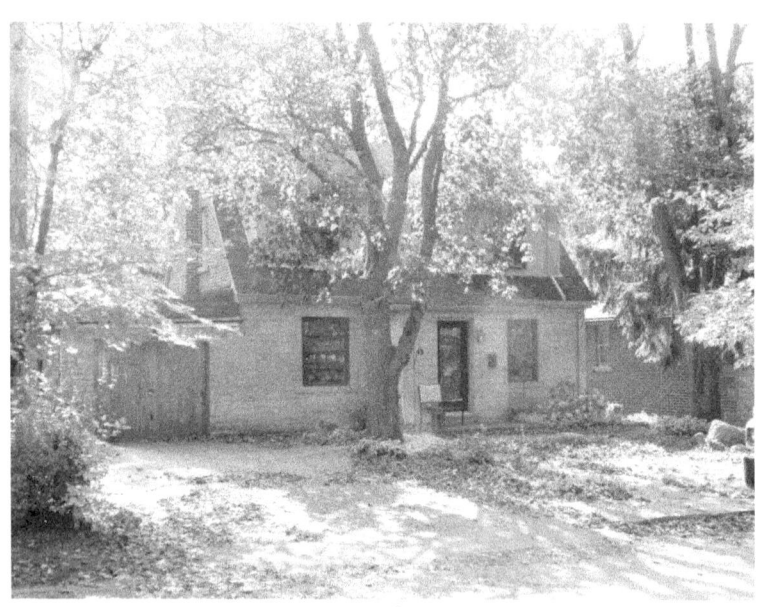

#13

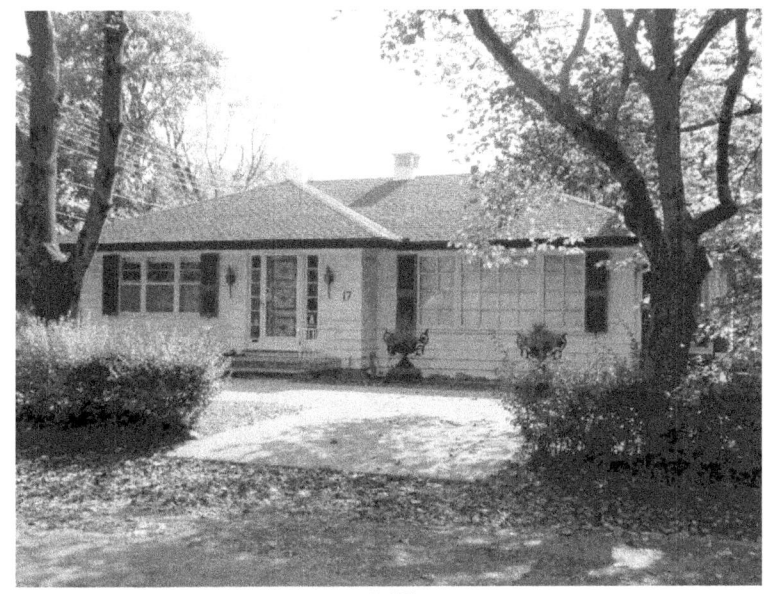

#17

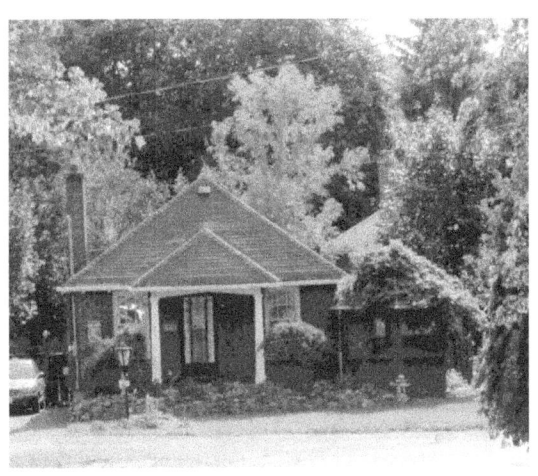

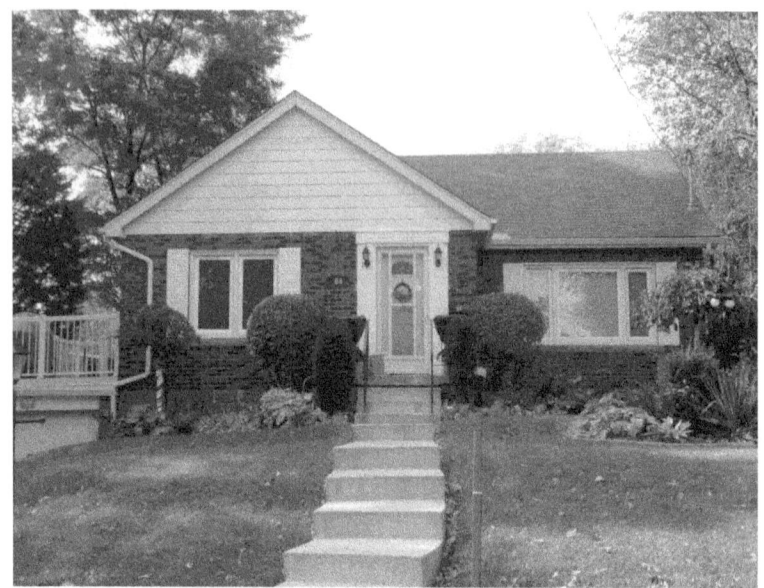

#64

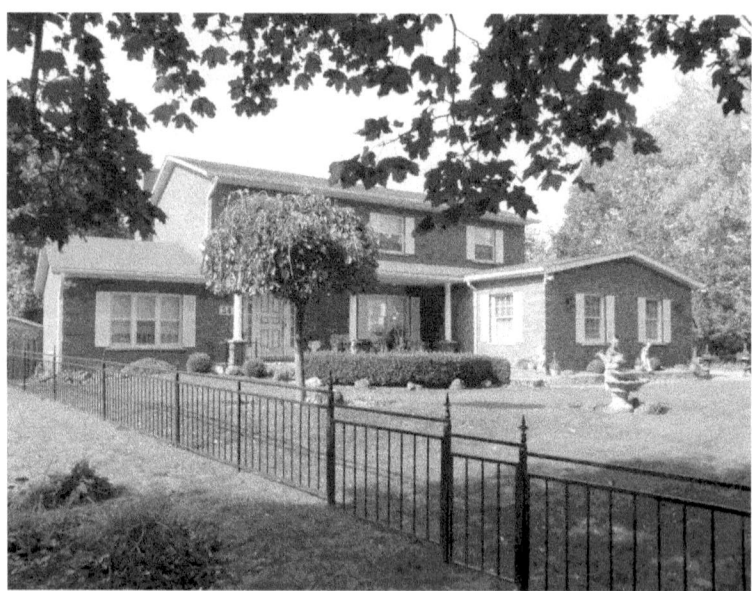

Valleyview 1978 - 54 East Street South

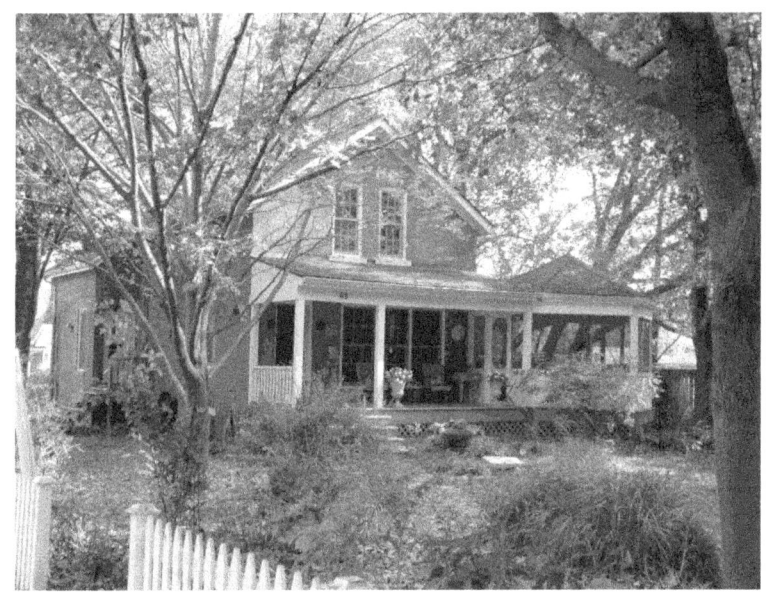

#69 Dunning Court

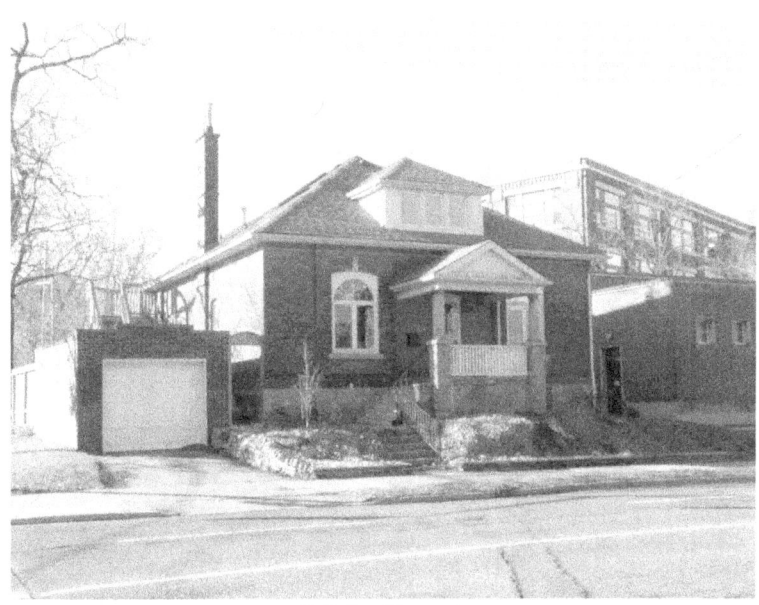

Main Street

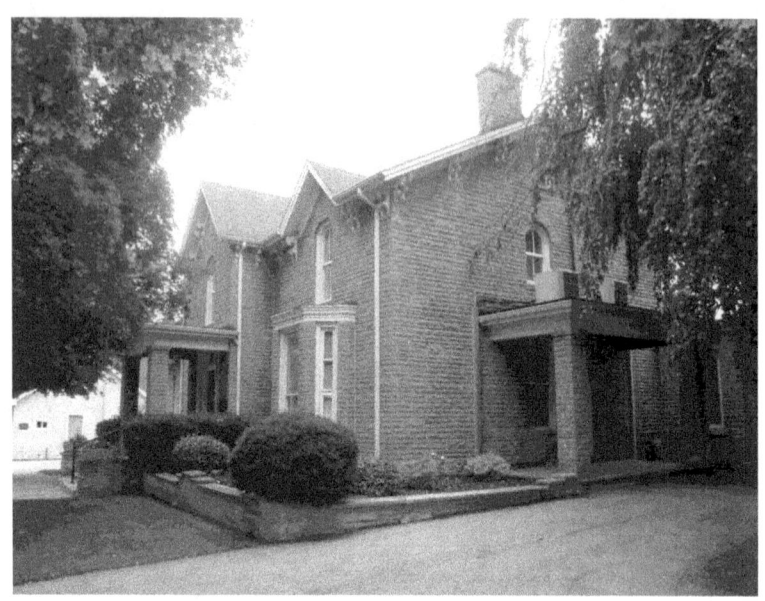

Cattel, Eaton and Chambers Funeral Home
53 Main Street

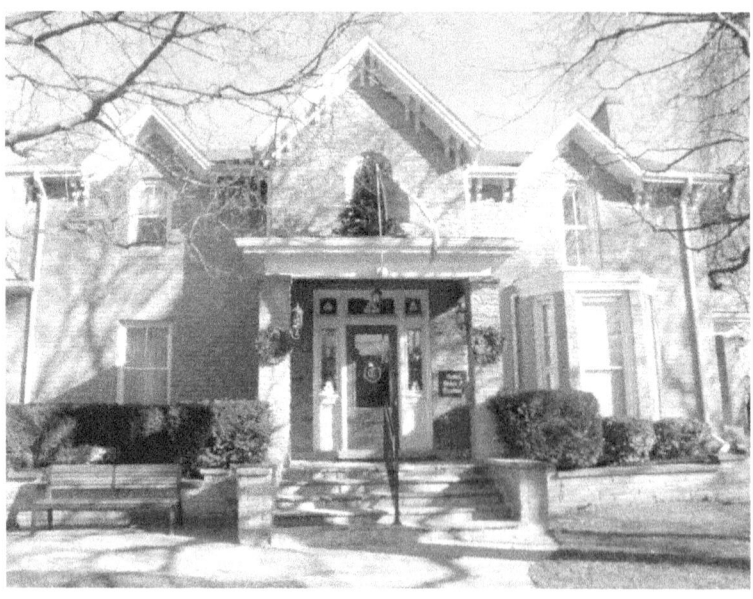

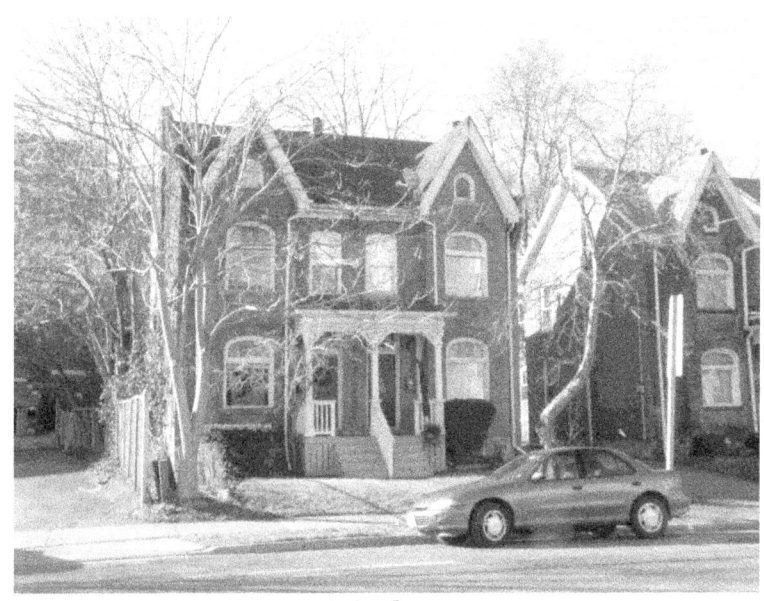

Main Street

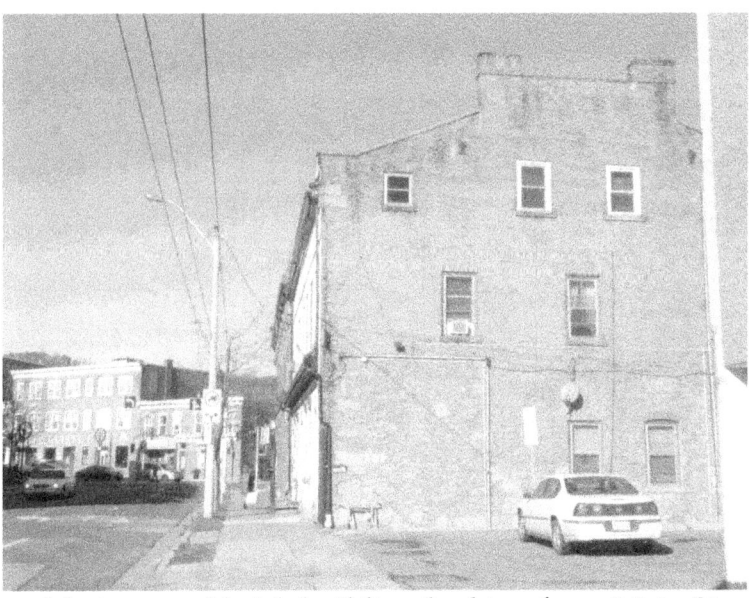

An old stone and brick building looking from Main Street
towards King Street

Grant Boulevard and area

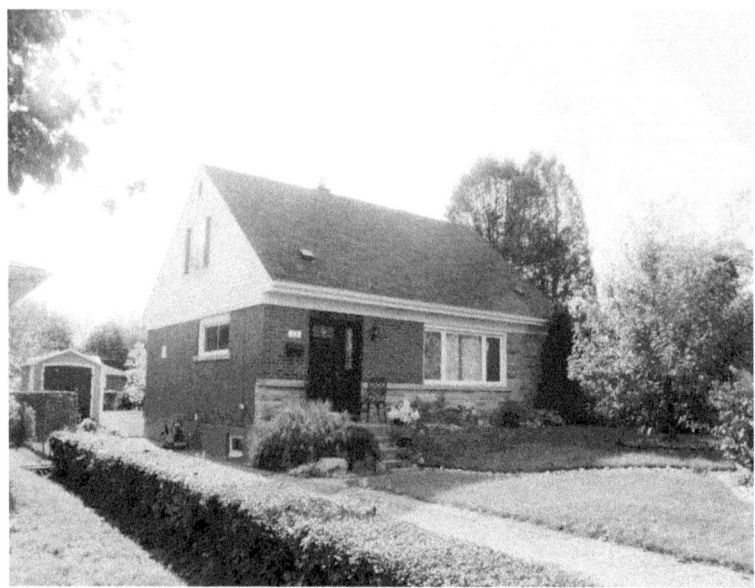

15 Grant Boulevard

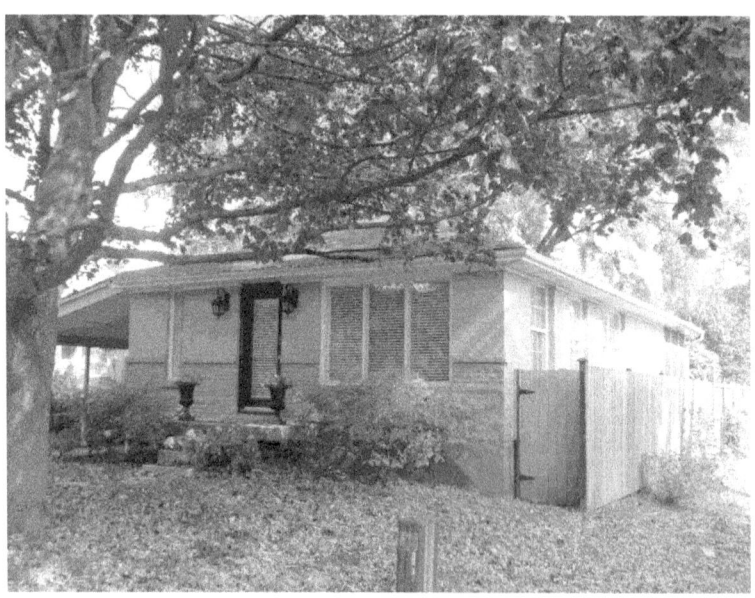

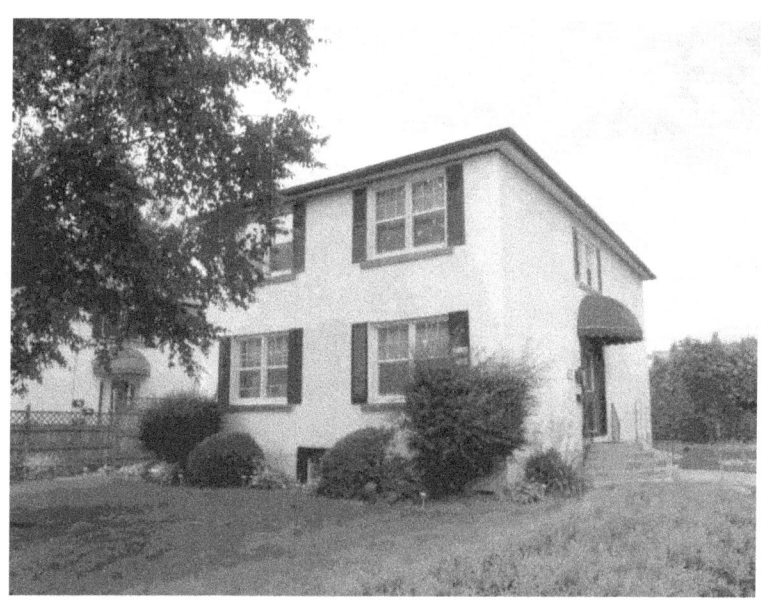

11 Don Street

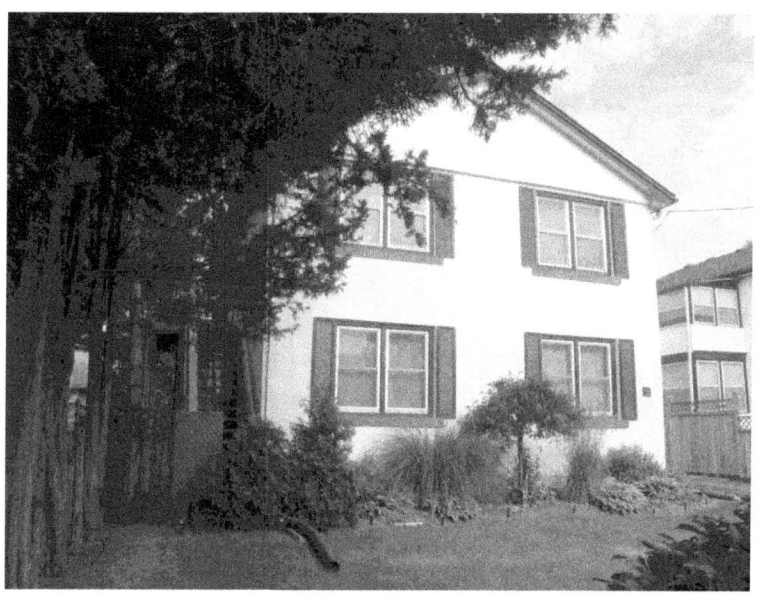

9 Don Street

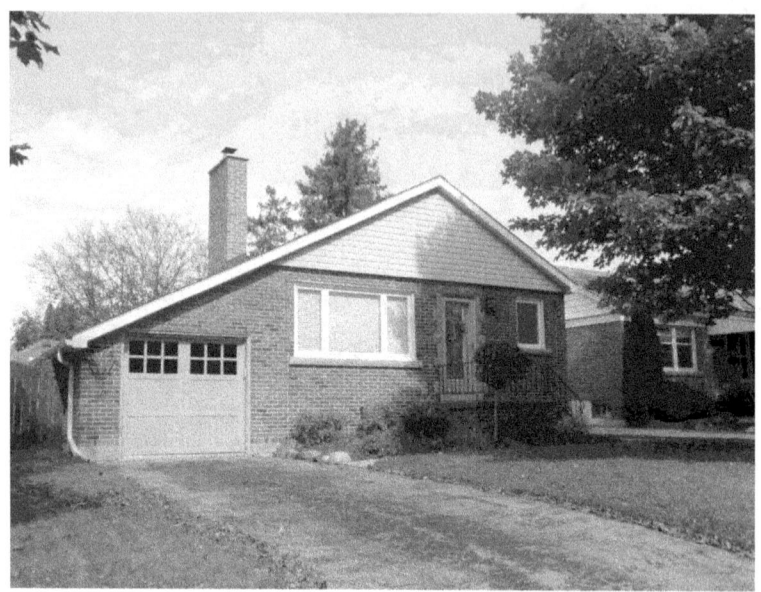

16 Grant Boulevard

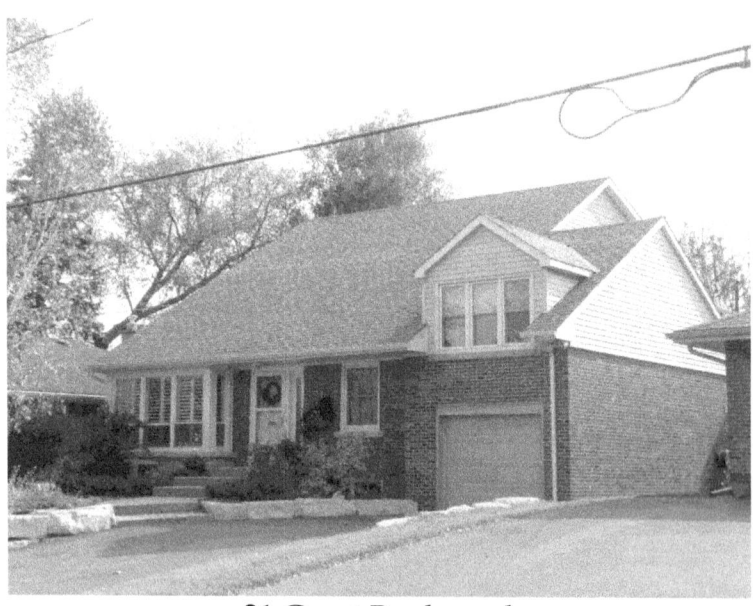

21 Grant Boulevard

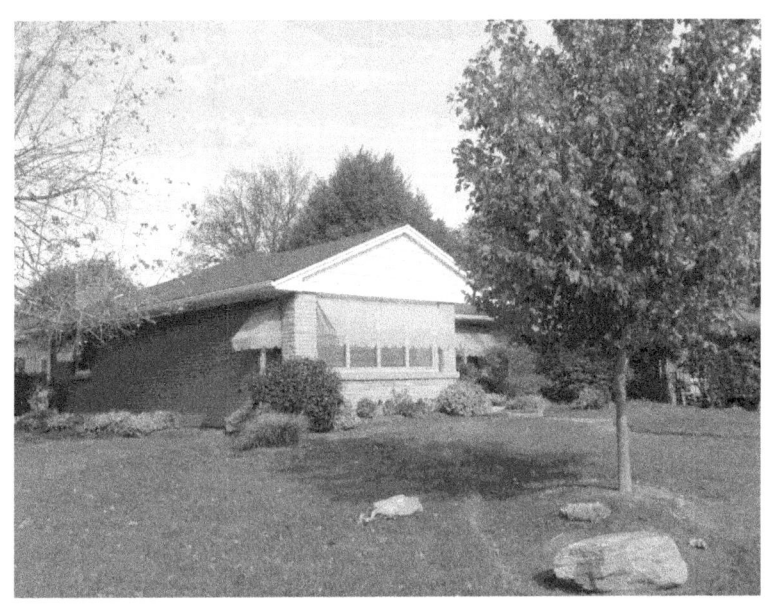

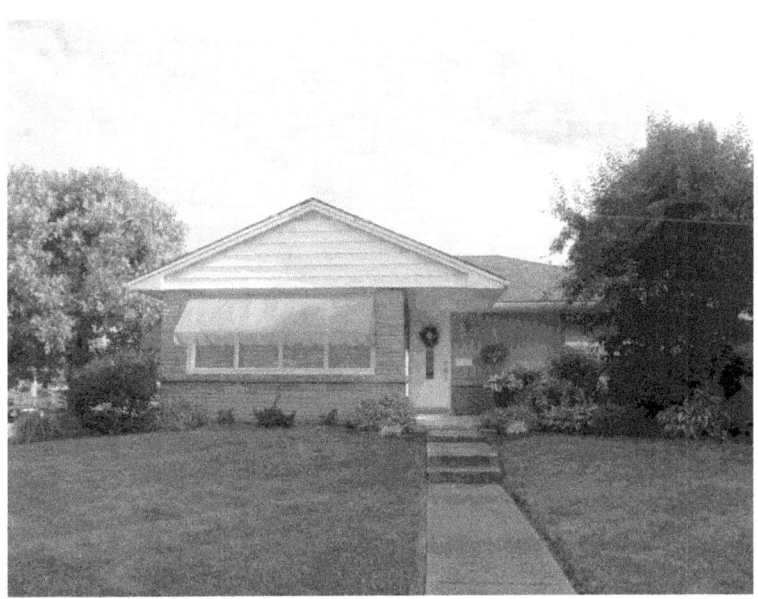

26 Grant Boulevard

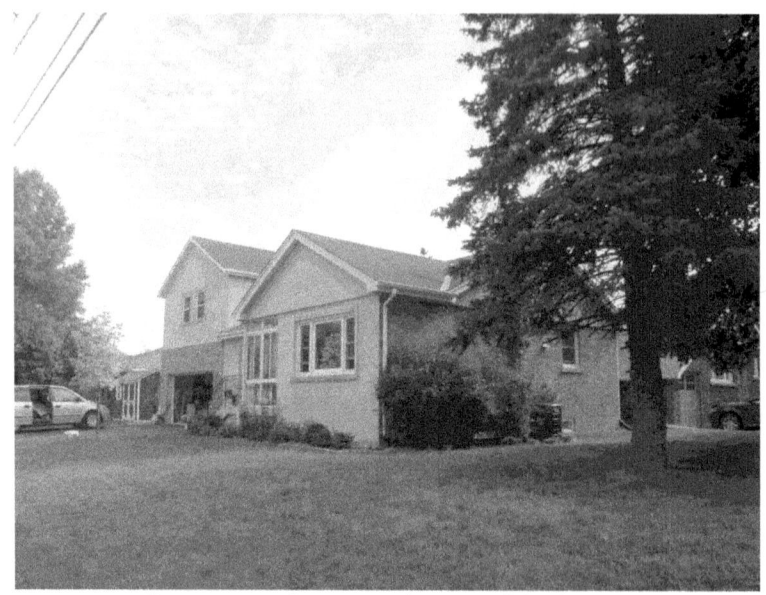

Garage and room above added 2010

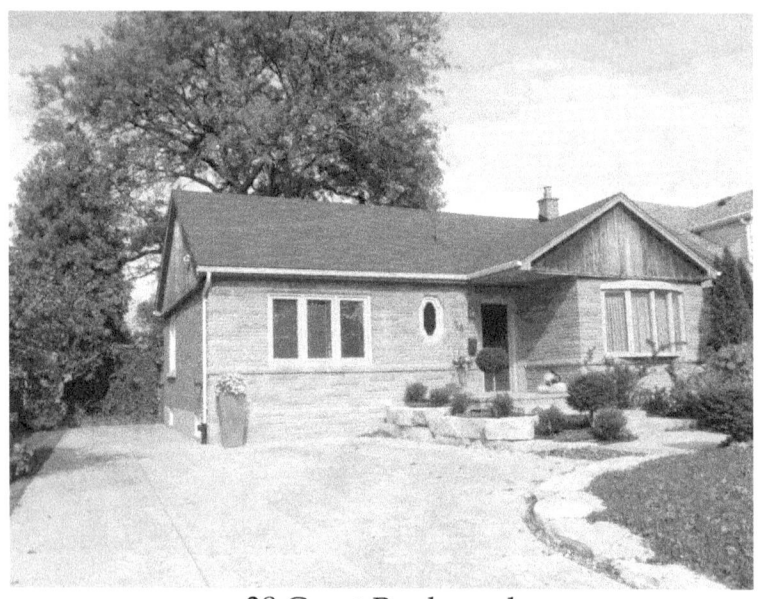

38 Grant Boulevard

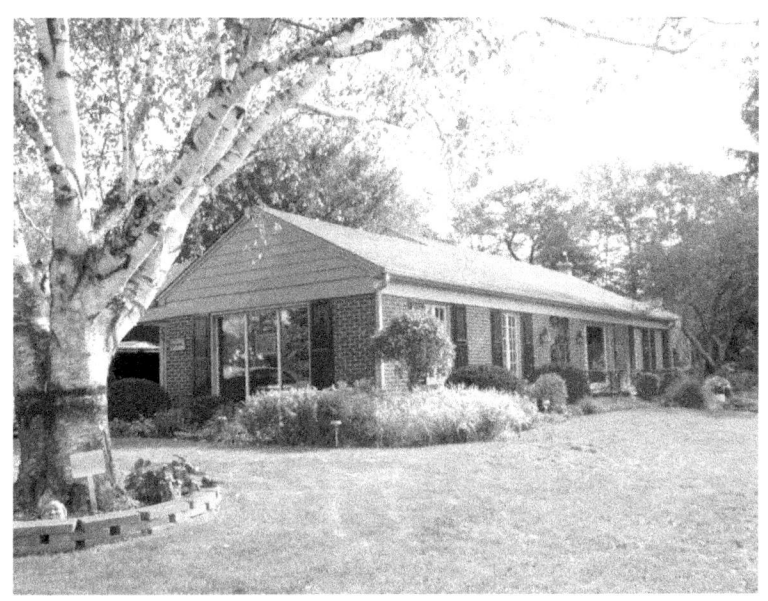

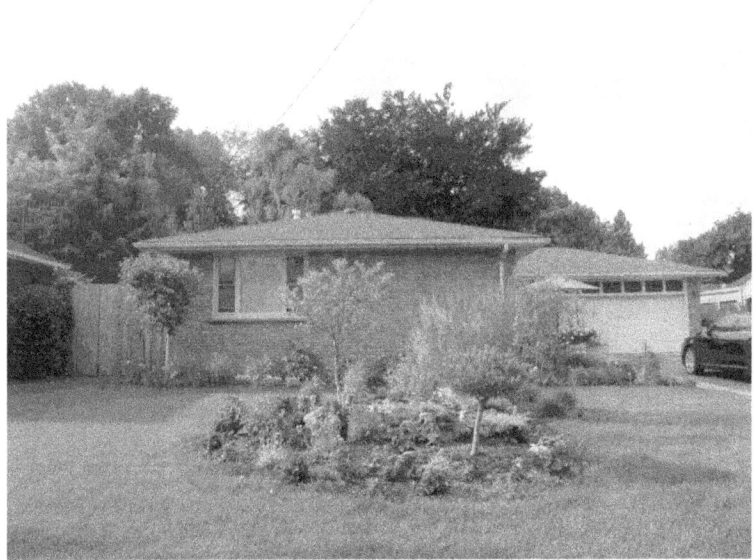

47 Grant Boulevard

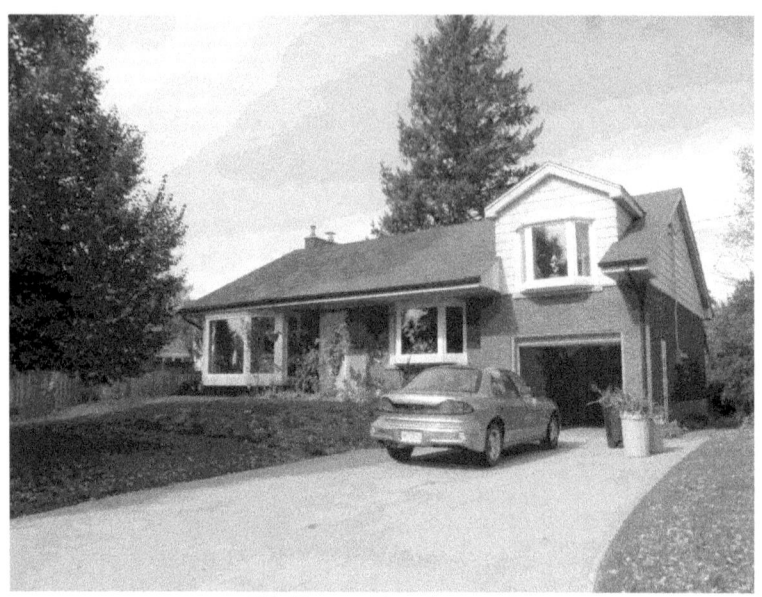

50 Grant Boulevard

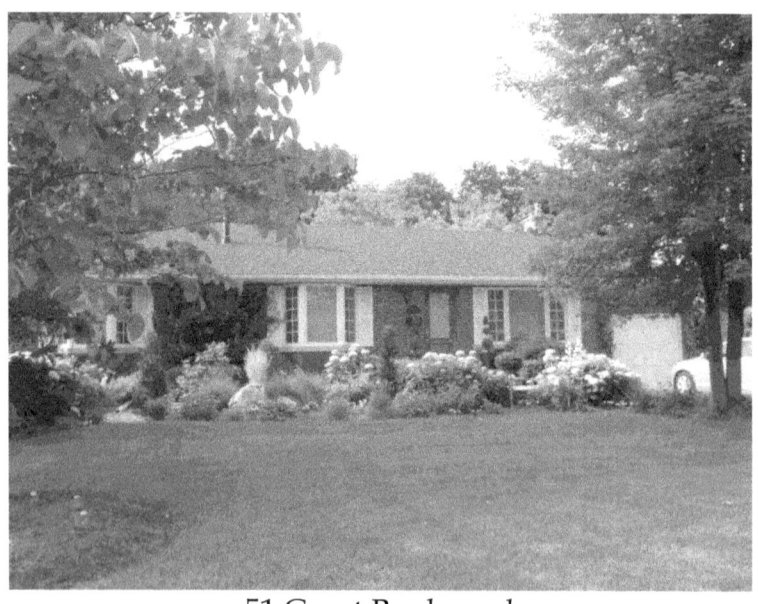

51 Grant Boulevard

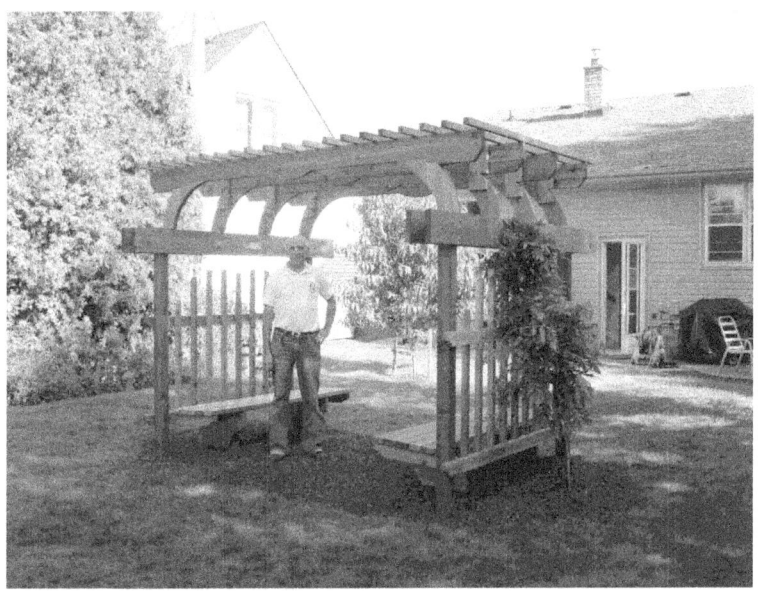

Arbour Harry built at 52 Grant Boulevard in 2005
Blue siding of house to the right of the picture

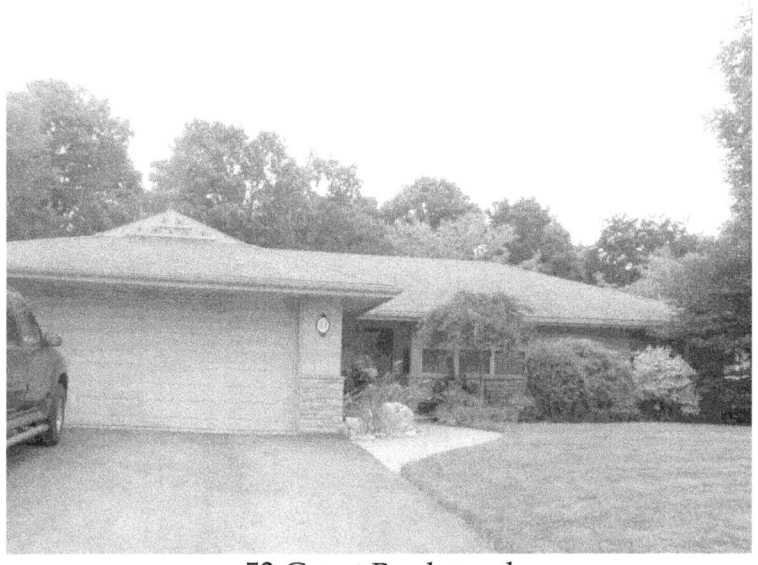

53 Grant Boulevard

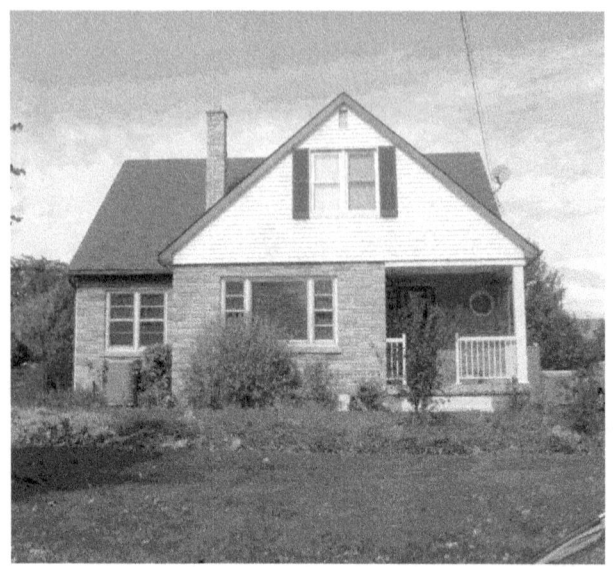

54 Grant Boulevard

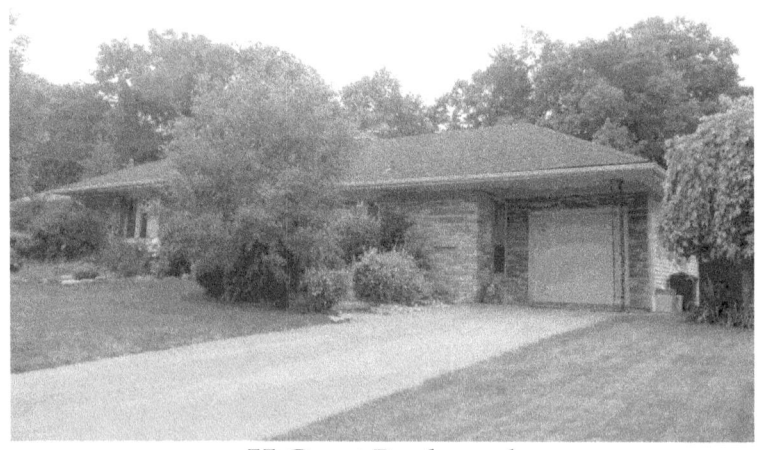

55 Grant Boulevard

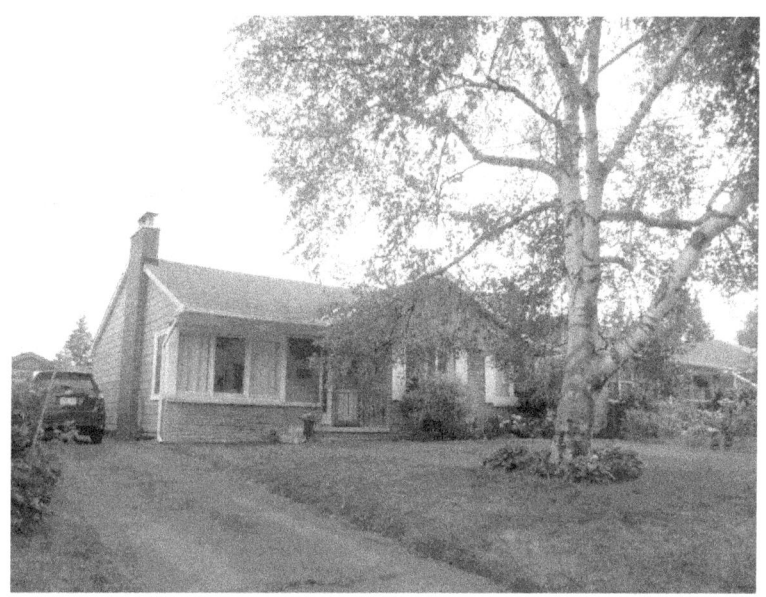

58 Grant Boulevard

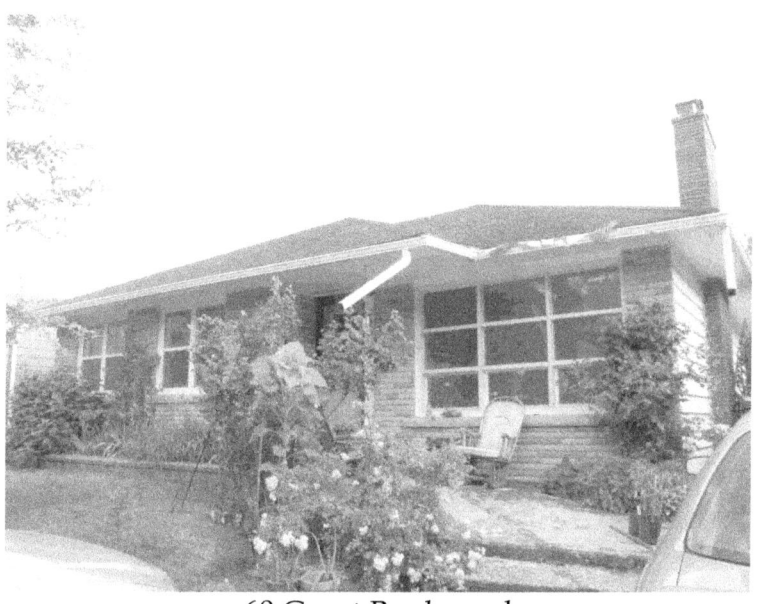

60 Grant Boulevard

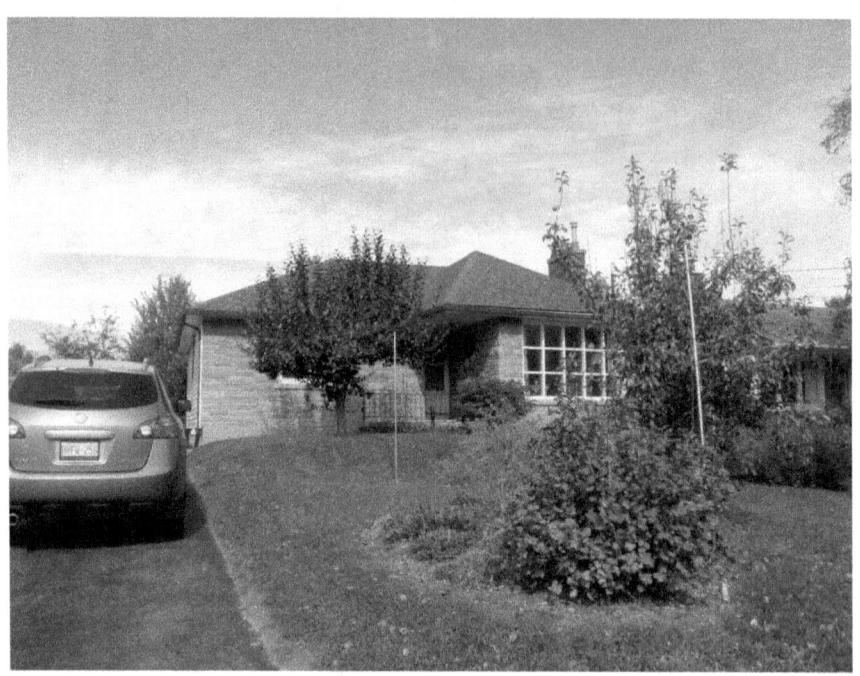

56 Grant Boulevard
Home of the Raues since August 2000
Built in 1953, one floor, three bedrooms, full basement

We added a vegetable garden in the backyard, raspberry, blueberry, black currant, red currant and gooseberry bushes, two pear trees and a cherry tree, as well as expanding the flower gardens.

www.ingramcontent.com/pod-product-compliance
Lightning Source LLC
Chambersburg PA
CBHW051329170526
45166CB00002B/734